BAC
ONE-ELEVEN

Cover:
BAC One-Eleven Series 409 G-AXBB of British Island
Airways. David Clark – British Aerospace, Weybridge

MODERN CIVIL AIRCRAFT:5
BAC ONE-ELEVEN

M.J.Hardy

LONDON

IAN ALLAN LTD

Contents

First published 1985

ISBN 0 7110 1486 8

Published by Ian Allan Ltd, Shepperton, Surrey; and printed by Ian Allan Printing Ltd at their works at Coombelands in Runnymede, England.

Below:
The first two Aloha Airlines One-Eleven 215s, N11181 and N11182. The Alohajets, as they were called, flew inter-island services from Honolulu in competition with Hawaiian Airlines' DC-9s. *Camera Hawaii via BAC*

Below right:
G-BGKE was the first of the three One-Eleven 539s ordered by British Airways in 1978; these had a 'wide body' look cabin and Spey hush kits.

Introduction

The short-haul jet airliner is now so well established as part of air transport that its somewhat circuitous entry into the airline picture may now seem somewhat surprising in retrospect. The BAC One-Eleven, as the pioneer example in this field, did not start out as a Vickers design to succeed the very successful and widely used Viscount turboprop, but began life as Hunting Aircraft Ltd's H.107 project and, after Hunting came into the Vickers and BAC orbit, was developed through several stages into the BAC One-Eleven to fill exactly the need for a jet replacement for the Viscount. Yet this might not have happened at all but for the Government-inspired rationalisation of the British aircraft industry into two main groupings – those of BAC and Hawker-Siddeley – that followed in the wake of the controversial 1957 Defence White Paper. The new jet project rapidly proved an attractive proposition to the airlines, and the first order from British United Airways was announced in May 1961.

It was soon evident that BAC had a winner in the One-Eleven, and there was unprecedented US airline interest in the type from a very early stage, soon confirmed by the first orders from Braniff and Mohawk. But it was the American Airlines order of July 1963 that really established the One-Eleven as a potential world-beater in airline eyes, for it came a bare three months after Douglas had decided to go ahead with the rival DC-9. This order, coming as it did from the very airline that had sponsored the famous DC-3 and several other important types, was a sensational commercial victory over Douglas and for a time it even seemed as if the DC-9 programme might be in jeopardy. Whereas the Viscount had sold to Capital Airlines Inc in 1954 and the Caravelle to United Air Lines six years later, at a time when the US aircraft industry had no competing turboprop or short-haul jet to offer, here was a British jet selling in the States in direct competition with an alternative and closely comparable US design, and selling against the hurdle of a 10% tariff barrier. And of course there was the natural reluctance of US airlines to forsake their own industry by ordering a foreign product.

Although BAC had to work from the disadvantage of a smaller potential home market for the One-Eleven and against the background of less intensive airline operations in Europe than in the USA, the One-Eleven went on to set an

outstanding record of in-service reliability, both in very intensive short-haul scheduled operations in the States and in the almost equally intensive area of peak-time European inclusive tour operations to Mediterranean and other holiday resort destinations. Some One-Elevens of US Air (formerly Allegheny Airlines Inc) have now logged more than 60,000 landings, or an average of 10 or 11 flights a day year in and year out since first entering Braniff or Mohawk service nearly 20 years ago; many airframes have now exceeded 60,000hr flying time. Before the short-haul jet, it was just not possible to get 11 or more revenue flights a day out of each aircraft, as the block times were too low and the turn-round times too long. Four design features in particular made the One-Eleven what one American Airlines executive called 'an instant aeroplane', able to achieve very quick turn-rounds on the ground and hence more revenue-earning time in the air. These were the forward and ventral airstairs for simultaneous passenger boarding, single-point pressure refuelling, baggage/freight holds at waist height for ease of loading, and the auxiliary power unit in the tail cone to provide engine starting and other services independently of ground vehicles.

The One-Eleven's splendid early success in the States and with European IT operators such as Laker Airways should really have led to plans for the stretched Series 500 maturing earlier than they did, ideally before the type first entered airline service, as was the case with the DC-9. But the year 1965, in which the One-Eleven made its debut in airline service, was a grim one for Britain's aircraft industry, with the TSR.2 and associated cancellations, uncertainty over the future of

Concorde (which itself was nearly cancelled), the aftermath of BOAC's controversial attempt the previous year to cancel its VC10 order, and the Plowden Committee on the aircraft industry. The new Labour Government, whose Prime Minister had so recently, when in Opposition, espoused the white heat of technology, seemed to distrust new technology; inside Labour's new white-coated technocrat image there was an old-fashioned Luddite struggling to get out. The result was that for some years thereafter the prevailing political climate was less than favourable to investment in new aerospace projects, and the Rolls-Royce bankruptcy of 1970 and the need to rescue the RB.211 family of engines absorbed funds that could otherwise have been used to develop the refanned Speys that were proposed for the One-Eleven 600 and 700 projects.

The One-Eleven had been made possible by the reshaping of the British aircraft industry but it was also in a very real sense a victim of another merger, that between BEA and BOAC to form British Airways, which led to the latter looking almost exclusively to Boeing for re-equipment, and finally to simply abandoning its role as a sponsor of new British airliners, without anyone in Government apparently understanding the significance or the implications of this. Too often money has been poured unthinkingly into the State airline without extracting any obligations in return, while the aircraft industry has been cold-shouldered, leaving a sizeable bill for the taxpayer to pick up. A good example of this was the plan announced in January 1984 to buy out the inflation-proof pension rights of 37,500 British Airways staff at an estimated cost of up to £150million – which would have more than paid for the fleet of One-Eleven 600s turned down by British Airways in 1978 in favour of an order for 18 Boeing 737-200s.

M. J. Hardy
Selsey, West Sussex

Below:
The first three One-Eleven 509s for Caledonian Airways Ltd were the first with the more powerful Spey 512-14DW engines and an increased maximum weight of 99,650lb for European inclusive tour operations; they seated 109 passengers. G-AWWX *Flagship Isle of Skye* **is seen here.**

Design Origins to First Flight

Whereas the piston-engined airliner started its life as a short-haul type and gradually, through progressive increases in size, developed over the years into long-range types with non-stop transcontinental or trans-oceanic capability, with the jet airliner this process worked in the reverse direction. It started as a long-haul type because it was over the longer hauls that the jet's speed, time-saving potential and ability to cruise in comfort at high altitudes had the most powerful passenger appeal and the strongest competitive impact on other airlines still flying propeller aircraft, and it was only fairly gradually that the advantages of pure jet travel percolated downwards to the shortest routes. Thus when air transport started in earnest after World War 1, straightforward passenger conversions of existing single-engined bombers, such as the Airco (de Havilland) DH.4A and DH.9C (seating two or three passengers where the rear gunner's position was), appeared; these were soon succeeded by slightly larger enclosed cabin developments such as the eight-passenger DH.18 and DH.34 types. Their twin-engined counterparts (also based on bombers), such as the Handley Page O/400 and W.8 series and the Vickers Vimy Commerical, flew the pioneer short-haul air routes between London, Paris and Brussels.

Airliner design shed its bomber heritage and started working its way upwards to bigger sizes and longer ranges, a process that was given great impetus by the competitive demands of the very important US transcontinental routes, especially those between New York and Los Angeles or San Francisco. Competition on these routes between the airlines themselves – American, United and TWA – and between the airlines and the transcontinental railroads, inspired a whole series of very important airliners in the 1930s aimed at cutting the coast-to-coast time and the number of stops on the route, working gradually towards the ideal of non-stop coast-to-coast service.

By September 1934 TWA was operating Douglas DC-2s between New York and Los Angeles taking some 16-18 hours each way, and American Airlines, to overcome the competitive disadvantages of its much slower routeing between these cities via Cleveland (which had no less than 15 stops between Cleveland and the west coast), sponsored a development of the DC-2 to take sleeper berths or up to 21 passengers in a slightly wider fuselage. This was the DST, or 'Douglas Sleeper Transport', the so-called 'day plane'

Below:
In its original form the Hunting H.107 had two 5,200lb st Bristol Orpheus 810 turbojets, and a tapered fin and rudder with the tailplane mounted half way up. When Hunting became a subsidiary of BAC the design was revised and its designation changed to BAC.107 (seen here in an artist's impression); the type now had two 7,350lb st Bristol BS.75 turbofans, a wider fuselage to seat five-abreast and the tailplane moved up to the top of the fin and rudder.

version of which was the famous DC-3, which became the world's most widely used airliner. American began DC-3 services between New York and Los Angeles in September 1936 over a more southerly routeing than before, with three or four stops, and TWA did not really recover its lead until July 1940 when it introduced the pressurised Boeing 307 Stratoliner, the first of the new generation four-engined airliners, on to the route, but still with three stops. TWA lost its lead temporarily when the Stratoliners were requisitioned for military service as C-75s early in 1942, but regained it in February 1946 when it introduced Lockheed Model 049 Constellation services between New York and Los Angeles, usually with two or three traffic stops although some crack flights had only one refuelling stop. In October 1953 TWA inaugurated the first truly non-stop flights between the two cities with Model 1049C Super Constellations, followed a month later by American Airlines with Douglas DC-7 non-stop services over the same route, and later still by United DC-7s.

The de Havilland Comet 1 was really a short/medium-haul airliner (by today's standards) operating long-haul routes, just as the Douglas DC-3 had been before it. BOAC's pioneering London-Johannesburg Comet service, which inaugurated the age of jet air travel on 2 May 1952, was flown with stops at Rome, Beirut (later Cairo), Khartoum, Entebbe (Uganda) and Livingstone (Northern Rhodesia); on this and the later Comet 1 routes to Colombo, Singapore and Tokyo introduced in 1952 and 1953 there were only a few

stage lengths of over 1,300 miles and most were in fact less than 1,000 miles. These were to be very much the sort of stage lengths the One-Eleven began operating over 12 years later; British United's first One-Eleven service, between London and Genoa (638 miles), was not dissimilar in length to BOAC's first Comet 1 sector, London-Rome (892 miles), although of course with the One-Eleven there was a much greater bias towards the truly short-haul stages.

The Comet 1, like its piston-engined contemporaries the Douglas DC-6B and Lockheed Model 749A Constellation, was regarded as essentially a long-haul type, and for a time it was widely believed that on distances of up to 500 miles or so the jet's superior speed did not result in much of a time-saving advantage, due not least to the need to climb to and descend from cruising height. But this argument ignored the tremendous passenger appeal the jet had already shown with Comet operators like BOAC, and it became more and more clear that there was a place for the jet even on the shortest routes that had hitherto been the preserve of turboprops like the Viscount.

The year 1956 saw the emergence of the truly short-haul jet airliner, with Capital Airlines Inc (which had pioneered Viscount services in the States two years before) ordering 10 of a short-haul variant of the Comet, the Mk 4A (plus four Comet 4s), and Air France placing the first order for 12 SNCASE SE.210 Caravelle jets in February that year, an order which was later doubled. The Comet 4A could have carried up to 92 tourist-class or over 70 first-class passengers in a fuselage 3ft 4in longer

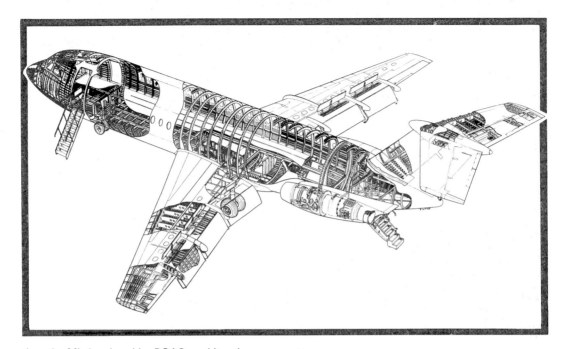

Above:
Cutaway drawing of a One-Eleven.

Above left:
This view shows the Fowler-type flaps lowered and the lift spoiler/air brakes raised; new low drag flap track fairings were introduced on the One-Eleven 500.

than the Mk 4 ordered by BOAC, and its wing span was reduced by 7ft to 108 ft to increase speed at lower altitudes. The Mk 4A was not in the end built because Capital's later financial difficulties, which led to its takeover by United in 1961, compelled it to cancel the order, but this variant was developed into the Comet 4B for BEA. This had a 6ft 6in longer fuselage than the Mk 4 and could seat up to 102 passengers, the wing pinion tanks of the Mk 4 and 4A being removed. BEA began Comet 4B services between London and Moscow on 1 April 1960, and the Mk 4B was also used by Olympic Airways.

The Caravelle was notable in being the first short/medium-haul airliner designed to have turbojets, and for setting a new fashion in rear-mounted engines, this layout giving an aerodynamically clean wing unbroken by nacelles or pylons, a much quieter cabin, and asymetric thrust problems with one engine out being minimised with this layout. The Caravelle more than any other civil type established the postwar French aircraft industry as a major force in world markets, and the type was to be operated by every European national airline outside the Communist bloc except BEA, KLM and Lufthansa, as well as by United in the States. The type had its origins in a specification of November 1951 issued by the French government agency SGACC for a *moyen courrier* (or medium-range airliner) for routes in the French Empire, especially between Paris and North Africa. For the latter a payload of 6-7 tonnes over stage lengths of 1,000 to 1,200 miles at a block speed of over 380mph was envisaged, thus enabling two Paris-North Africa return journeys to

be flown in 24hr. Air France began Caravelle services between Paris and Istanbul on 6 May 1959, and the type seated typically about 64 passengers in a two-class interior or a maximum of 99 tourist-class. The lengthened Caravelle 10B or Super Caravelle seats from 68 to 105 passengers and, like the further stretched Caravelle 12, which can take up to 140 charter or IT passengers, has more powerful Pratt & Whitney JT8D turbofans in place of the Rolls-Royce RA.29 Avons of most earlier versions.

The Hunting H.107

As well as the first orders for the Caravelle and short-haul Comet, the year 1956 saw the beginnings of the airliner that was later to become the BAC One-Eleven. In May of that year Hunting Aircraft Ltd completed a design study for a small jet airliner known as the H.107 (originally as the P.107), seating 32 to 48 passengers four-abreast and with a range of up to 1,000 miles and a cruising speed of 400kt. When the design was first schemed the

Right:
This rear end view of Aloha Airlines One-Eleven 215 N11182 shows the hydraulically-operated ventral air-stairs lowered and details of the variable-incidence tailplane. Note how the auxiliary power unit jet pipe at the end of the tailcone is upturned to prevent the exhaust impinging on other aircraft.

Far right:
The forward passenger door with power-operated air-stairs in the stowed position.

choice of suitable jet engines for such an aeroplane was severely limited, a factor that had for some time deterred any ideas of building a small jet for the truly short-haul routes. The powerplant finally chosen was the Bristol Orpheus, intended as a simple and reliable successor to such early postwar turbojets as the Rolls-Royce Nene; this had made its first test bed run in December 1954 and the next year first flew in the Folland Gnat light fighter. The H.107 had two 5,200lb st Bristol BOr3/5 Orpheus 810 jets in rear-mounted nacelles like the Caravelle; by 1959 a later and more powerful version of this engine, the 7,150lb st BOr12B Orpheus which was a civil variant of the military BOr12, was specified for the H.107.

The H.107 had a low wing with a moderate sweepback of 20° at the quarter-chord line to allow operation from short runways and to avoid the need for complex high-lift devices. The H.107 originally had the tailplane half way up the fin and a more tapered fin and rudder than the One-Eleven, and instead of the latter's ventral airstairs there was at first a passenger door in the port side just aft of the wing trailing edge, as well as another one aft of the flight deck, the galley and two toilets being situated aft. The H.107's original basic specification had been modified after discussions with airline operators in a number of countries to give an all-up weight of 41,500lb (less than half that of the One-Eleven 200), a balanced field length of 5,000ft and an optimum stage length of 700 to 800 nautical miles. The engines were mounted behind the rear pressure bulkhead, thus keeping the pressure cabin outside the cones of noise and jet efflux, and silencers or thrust reversers could be fitted if required, as well as water injection for power restoration under 'hot and high' conditions.

Serious design work on the H.107 had begun in November 1957, low-speed wind-tunnel tests were made and a full-scale wooden mock-up was built; in mid-1958 it was estimated that development costs for the H.107 would be between £4million and £5million including production tooling, a sum which would have necessitated a joint co-operative effort with another company, and the selling price would have been about £250,000 with the break-even number reached with 90 aircraft built. At this stage the H.107 was smaller than the One-Eleven 200, with a span of 80ft, length of 77ft 9in (nearly 16ft less than the Series 200), and a wing area of 800sq ft. Cabin length excluding the flight deck was 19ft, one-third that of the One-Eleven 200, and maximum internal cabin width was 102in, compared to 124in for the Series 200. Baggage capacity was 388cu ft for the 40-seater version, of which 225cu ft was above the cabin floor.

In September 1958, to improve on the economics of the Orpheus version, the H.107 design was revised around two new Bristol turbofans, the BE.61 of some 7,000lb st, which was redesignated BS.61 after the formation of Bristol Siddeley Engines Ltd in April 1959, and the 7,350lb st BS.75 engine. At the same time the registration G-APOH was reserved by Hunting Aircraft Ltd for the H.107, and this would have been applied to the prototype had it been built. With the new engines the H.107 could now seat from 48 to 56 passengers, and the take-off weight of 42,400lb with two BS.61s was now close to that of the Convair 440 and Fokker F.27 Friendship, two of the types which the H.107 was intended to replace on short-haul routes. Early in 1960 the BS.75's specific fuel consumption at maximum thrust was revealed as 0.5lb/hr/lb thrust,

which made it the lowest announced for any jet engine up to that time; this would have made it especially attractive to H.107 customers, as it would have enabled them to offer a real competitive threat to rival turboprop-equipped airlines. The prototype BS.75 engine first ran on the test bed on 6 February 1962, but only a few months later development of this promising turbofan was suspended, no doubt partly to enable Bristol Siddeley to concentrate all its resources on the BS.53 Pegasus for the Hawker P.1127 Kestrel and Harrier, and the BS.100 for the supersonic Hawker P.1154. The firm was also in the throes of industrial reorganisation, having announced the takeover of the de Havilland Engine Co and Blackburn Engines Ltd in November 1961.

Hunting Aircraft Ltd was to suffer the same fate after the formation of the British Aircraft Corporation Ltd in February 1960 to bring together the aircraft and guided weapons interests of Bristol, English Electric and Vickers Ltd; the new BAC acquired a controlling share interest in Hunting Aircraft Ltd, which as a result became an operating subsidiary and later, with effect from 1 January 1964, BAC's Luton Division. Early in 1960 the Vickers civil aircraft development group prepared a report on the H.107 for the board of Vickers-Armstrongs (Aircraft) Ltd, and in May that year a Hunting Aircraft team led by the firm's managing director, Mr Arthur Summers, visited Weybridge to make a presentation of the H.107 to a Vickers team headed by Sir George Edwards, and from then on the project went forward as a joint Vickers-Hunting effort.

At that time Vickers did not have a jet airliner project of its own which could directly replace the Viscount on the short/medium-haul routes, as the company's efforts had been concentrated on the long-haul VC10 for BOAC. As a companion for this on the medium-haul routes Vickers had prepared the VC11 project (also known as the Vickers Type 1400), which was basically a scaled-down derivative of the VC10 with four Rolls-Royce RB.163/11 Spey turbofans in the same rear-mounted configuration as the VC10. It would have seated up to 138 passengers and was intended for routes of between 1,000 and 2,500 miles, the maximum gross weight being 170,000lb and cruising speed 600mph. Had it been built it would have been competing with the Convair 880 and 990A, and the Boeing 720 and 727; as Convair's very heavy losses on the 880/990A programme were to show in a few years, this was already an overcrowded sector of the market. There was some airline interest in the VC11 project, especially from Trans-Canada Airlines (now Air Canada), but the fact that BEA had already ordered the DH Trident, future versions of which would be directly competitive with the VC11, and that BOAC, heavily committed to the VC10, had no requirement for its smaller companion, finally caused the VC11 project to be discontinued early in 1961.

So when Hunting came into the BAC and Vickers orbit, it made much more sense to develop the H.107 into what was to be the One-Eleven, making use of Vickers' unrivalled experience in short-haul turbine transport with the Viscount, of which 444 were eventually built. By 1967 Viscounts had flown over 7,750,000 hours in service and were operating with over 40 airlines, eight Governments and 13 business corporations in over 30 countries. With this background it was perhaps surprising that the idea of a short-haul jet took rather long to reach maturity, but apart from the lack of a suitable engine mentioned previously, the jet's higher capital cost could only be justified if the airlines could make full use of its higher productivity by achieving a high utilisation with it: with many short-haul routes subject to competition among several airlines or seasonal traffic variations and, especially in Europe, to bad weather in the winter months, it was not always easy to achieve high utilisation and frequency of service and so justify the purchase of jets for a short-haul network. Indeed for a time in mid-1960 it seemed as if the best hope for getting the H.107 into production lay in developing it initially as a Vickers Valetta and Varsity replacement for the RAF, a role later filled by the DH.125 Dominie T Mk 1. A proposal for such a variant of the H.107, initially powered by Bristol Orpheus jets in the interests of rapid development, and which could have been fitted at a later stage with the more economic BS.75 turbofans, was in fact put to the Government but did not get a positive reaction, and so development of the H.107 with two BS.75s continued as a civil type.

Table 1

From H.107 to One-Eleven 200

	H.107	H.107	BAC.107	One-Eleven
Date	mid-1958	Sept 1959	Sept 1960	mid-1961
Engines	5,200lb st	7,150lb st	7,350lb st	10,400lb st
	BOr3/5	BOr12B	BS.75	Spey 505-14
	Orpheus 810	Orpheus		
Passengers	32-48	48	59	69
Span	80ft	80ft	81ft 8in	88ft 6in
Length	77ft 9in	85ft 2in	84ft	92ft 1in
Wing area	800sq ft	800sq ft	825sq ft	980sq ft
Basic operating wt	20,670lb	22,133lb		
Max payload	10,960lb	12,000lb	12,000lb	14,000lb
Max gross wt	41,500lb	44,900lb	48,500lb	68,250lb
Max landing wt	39,500lb	–	46,000lb	65,000lb
Max zero fuel wt	31,630lb	–	41,000lb	58,000lb
Cruising speed	461mph	461mph	507mph at 30,000ft	540mph at 25,000ft
Range	1,094 miles with full payload; 2,300 miles with 3,100lb payload	– –	500 miles with full payload	1,220 miles with full payload

At this time, among the first of several important design changes made under Vickers direction, the H.107's fuselage was widened to take five-abreast seating like the Viscount, and the tailplane was moved up to the top of the fin. Cabin length was now 48ft 8in with more windows (26 down each side), an internal width of 10ft, and there was seating for up to 59 economy-class passengers, or 50 first-class (four-abreast). In August 1960 a further presentation of the H.107 in this revised form was made at Weybridge to Bristol, Hunting and Vickers sales and technical personnel, and this was immediately followed by exploratory sales visits by BAC teams to major airlines all over the world to assess their interest in the H.107, now known as the BAC.107, and to get their reactions to its design and operational features. Among the operators visited was Trans-Australia Airlines, to whose management the BAC team made a presentation of a possible joint VC11 and BAC.107 fleet for their future jet requirements, a similar proposal being made to TAA's major competitor on Australian domestic routes, Ansett-ANA. TAA was impressed by these proposals and liked the BAC.107, although it had reservations about the untried nature of the BS.75 turbofan, even though this did embody design experience from other Bristol engines such as the Proteus, Olympus and the BS.53. Ansett-ANA was later interested in the One-Eleven with long-range centre-section tank-age, this being offered with low-pressure tyres for operating from Melbourne Essendon airport, but eventually both it and TAA ordered Douglas DC-9 Series 30s.

In the last quarter of 1960 a number of design changes were made to the BAC.107 based on airline reactions to the visits by BAC sales teams. A conventional hydraulic system for such equipment as the undercarriage and flaps replaced the previous pneumatic one and, to meet airline demands for increased freight and baggage capacity, the fuselage cross-section was changed from a circular one to a double-bubble one of two intersecting circles with the floor forming the common chord line; later, a change back was made in April 1961 to a circular but larger cross-section. By the beginning of 1961 a number of airlines were firmly interested in the BAC.107, but there was a divergence in their requirements, one group of potential customers accepting the type virtually as it was, and placing most emphasis on simplicity and low capital cost, while the other group of airlines, although liking the concept behind the BAC.107, wanted improvements in performance, payload and equipment which would not have been possible within the required timescale with the BS.75 turbofan, which had yet to make its first test bed runs. This latter group of airlines represented potential orders for a larger number of aircraft, and attached greater importance than the first group to early delivery.

This, together with the untried nature of the BS.75, led BAC to change to two 9,850lb st Rolls-Royce RB.163 Spey turbofans, the same engine that was to power the de Havilland DH.121 Trident for BEA, and in March 1961 this new version was designated BAC.111 or, as it very quickly became known, the BAC One-Eleven. The

Left:
This rear view of a BUA One-Eleven 501 shows the reverse thrust cascade apertures in the top of each engine cowling and the stub fairings carrying the engines, also the upturned APU exhaust.

BAC.107 did in fact remain on offer to the airlines until Bristol-Siddeley decided to stop BS.75 development and, had it been ordered in sufficient quantities, it would have followed the Spey version about a year later. It would have had a slightly shorter fuselage than the One-Eleven 200, thinner metal skin gauges and a reduced fuel capacity.

The more powerful Speys enabled the One-Eleven's fuselage to be made two seat rows longer; it could now seat up to 69 passengers five-abreast at 37in seat pitch in an all-economy interior, or 57 mixed class with 28 first-class passengers in four-abreast seats at 28in pitch and 29 economy class five-abreast at 36in pitch. Maximum take-off weight had now gone up to 68,250lb for the standard version, or 73,500lb with long-range centre-section tankage; by September 1962 the standard version's gross weight was 73,500lb and engine thrust was now 10,400lb st from the Spey 505-14s, while maximum seating capacity in a high-density layout grew to 79 by the time of the first flight. Table 1 shows how this short-haul jet grew in stages between its inception as the twin-Orpheus H.107 to its final eve-of-first flight form as the twin-Spey One-Eleven.

Go-Ahead and First Order

In March 1961 at a technical meeting at Weybridge agreement was reached on over 50 basic points to be incorporated in the One-Eleven design. That same month a BAC board meeting took the decision to go ahead with both the One-Eleven and the BAC.107, and to begin an initial production batch of 20 of the former to meet target delivery dates of autumn 1964; a second a batch of 20 was commenced in the spring of 1962. With the go-ahead given, Sir George Edwards began to direct the build-up within BAC of the organisation needed to design, develop, sell and produce both the One-Eleven and the BAC.107; the One-Eleven was in fact the first wholly new project to be tackled by the recently-formed British Aircraft Corporation as a unified and integrated enterprise.

As befitted the design's origins, a number of senior Hunting Aircraft men were given important positions in the One-Eleven organisation. Overall responsibility was carried by Sir George Edwards, with Mr A. W. E. Houghton, assistant managing director of Vickers-Armstrongs (Aircraft), responsible to him for the overall programme. Mr Arthur Summers, managing director of Hunting Aircraft, was in charge of all aspects of development and Mr B. Stephenson, director of engineering for Vickers-Armstrongs (Aircraft), had technical responsibility for the programme, while Hunting's technical director, Mr F. Pollicutt, led the technical control and design co-ordination. Responsible to him for the integration of airline requirements into the design was Hunting's chief designer Mr A. J. K. Carline, who had been involved with the H.107.

The design and production effort was split up as follows: BAC Hurn was to produce the front and centre fuselage and the systems, as well as undertaking the final assembly and the modifying of One-Elevens to customer requirements. BAC Weybridge undertook major components such as wing skins and fuselage panels, as well as producing the centre section and undercarriage.

BAC's Luton Division, which until December 1963 was Hunting Aircraft Ltd, undertook detail design and manufacture of the wings, ailerons and flaps; when this Division was closed in December 1966 its work at Luton was transferred to Weybridge. BAC Filton was responsible for One-Eleven rear fuselage and tail units.

Details of the One-Eleven were first announced to a wider public at a BAC press conference on 9 May 1961 at which the initial order for 10 aircraft was announced for his airline by Mr Freddie Laker, then executive director of British United Airways. The One-Eleven thus became the first postwar British airliner for which a British independent and not one of the state airlines placed the initial launching order; BUA also took an option on five more which would have been 'firmed up' if BUA had been granted the licences for European scheduled routes it had applied for earlier that year. As Sir George Edwards said at the conference, BAC could now say 'there you are, it is on the go. It is not just one of those things that we'll build if you'll buy it' and he also revealed that Mr Robert Six, the

president of Continental Airlines Inc of Denver, Colorado, one of the US domestic trunk airlines, had authorised him to say that it was sufficiently interested to send a team to England to evaluate the One-Eleven with the possibility of an order within 90 days. Also, two of the 13 US local service airlines, Ozark Air Lines Inc of St Louis, Missouri, and Frontier Airlines Inc of Denver, placed letters of intent for (respectively) five and six One-Eleven 200s. This marked an unprecedented level of American interest in a new British airliner at such an early stage, and it demonstrated how completely BAC had stolen a march on the US industry.

In the event Continental, which had ordered 15 Viscount 812s which began operations over its Chicago-Los Angeles route on 26 May 1958, postponed a decision on its short-haul jet and later ordered the DC-9, taking delivery of its first DC-9 Series 10F in March 1966. Frontier Airlines, largest of the US local service carriers, in 1961 serving about 70 communities in 11 western states, decided on converting its Convair 340s to Allison

501 turboprop power as Convair 580s instead of ordering One-Elevens, and it did not introduce short-haul jets until 1969, when Boeing 737s entered service. Ozark Air Lines, which in 1961 served a network of 45 towns and cities in 10 mid-western states, likewise decided to postpone the purchase of short-haul jets, and the company's first DC-9 Series 15 was not delivered until mid-1966.

The first firm US order for the One-Eleven was announced by Braniff International Airways Inc, a major domestic and international operator, on 20 October 1961 for six One-Eleven 203s plus six on option to replace Convair 340s and 440s on domestic routes; this was especially significant as it was the first time a US airline had ordered a new British airliner almost off the drawing board. The second confirmed US customer was another local service carrier, Mohawk Airlines Inc of Utica, New York, which placed the first of several orders, for four One-Eleven 204s, on 24 July 1962. Mohawk operated a network in the eastboard seaboard states, and also to Toronto and Montreal in Canada; like Braniff, it had not had the benefit of previous Viscount operating experience to predispose it in the One-Eleven's favour.

It is interesting to recall that BUA was a comparatively late convert to the One-Eleven, and that as recently as January 1961 the airline had announced its readiness to buy five DH Tridents as well as four VC10s (it actually ordered three VC10 Type 1103s). Mr Freddie Laker gave several reasons for the change of heart when announcing the BUA One-Eleven order; he believed that 10 of the latter would give more flexibility than five Tridents, BUA's route pattern being such that if a Trident went unserviceable on a Saturday morning, that meant 20% of BUA's capacity lost, but only 10% with the One-Eleven. Secondly, although the One-Eleven was not as fast as the developed Trident, any time lost could be regained by the BAC jet's faster turn-round. Also the One-Eleven's noise level would be lower and field performance 'very much superior' to other types such as the Caravelle and Trident, and Mr Laker was convinced that BUA could operate the One-Eleven at a lower seat-mile cost than these types. Finally, because the One-Eleven was smaller BUA could offer the same personal cabin service, but BUA's main reason for choosing it was that it was, in Mr Laker's words, 'a straight 100% replacement for the Viscount'.

Thus, although BUA had not sponsored the One-Eleven in the sense that BEA had earlier sponsored the Viscount and Vanguard, by exerting a close influence on the design from the earliest stages or drawing up a detailed specification for it to fit, BUA had had 'a few things to say' (as Mr Laker put it) in the final form its new jet took. In particular, it had to be the same size as the

Viscount, operate non-stop between London and Malta against a 40kt wind with reserves (the design case) and had to operate to the same WAT (Weight, Altitude, Temperature) curve as the Viscount in 'hot and high' conditions. Also, the One-Eleven was to prove very suitable for the growing group charter and inclusive tour holiday traffic to Spain, Majorca, the Adriatic, Greece and North Africa which the British independent airlines and inclusive tour operators had done so much to develop. It was due not least to the group charter and IT holiday market that the One-Eleven became the first British postwar airliner for which the British independents, and not one of the State airlines, formed the major part of the home market; altogether 53 One-Elevens of all variants (almost a quarter of those built) were built to the order of British independents, and 12 more were acquired by them second-hand from foreign operators, while 21 One-Eleven 510s and 539s were built for British European Airways. In addition, several independent operators such as Dan-Air Services Ltd, Air UK and Air Manchester did not order any factory-new One-Elevens but built up their fleets through resales and by buying on the used airliner market.

Technical Description
Meanwhile, with the first order placed, the project now on a firm basis and with the first flight scheduled for the second quarter of 1963 and deliveries to BUA to begin in September 1964, detail design work gathered momentum.

The One-Eleven's fail-safe structure is of copper-based aluminium alloy for better stress corrosion resistance and fatigue-strength properties than aluminium-zinc alloy. Wing sweepback, as on the H.107, is 20° at the quarter-chord line both for structural simplicity and to avoid complex high-lift devices, while an aspect ratio of eight was chosen as the best compromise between the demands of low wing weight, high fuel stowage volume, minimum gust response and optimum climb performance. The wing torsion box is made up of three shear webs (ie spars) with integrally machined skin panels fastened on to stringers, and a number of ribs.

The ailerons are made of Redux-bonded light alloy honeycomb and are operated manually through servo tabs. The light alloy hydraulically-operated Fowler-type flaps are in three sections each side and on the One-Eleven 475 they are coated in glass fibre as protection from the poorer-grade runway surfaces from which this variant is specially intended to operate. There are two light alloy spoiler/air brakes on each wing upper surface, an inner one and an outer one each side ahead of the flaps, being separated by the centre flap track fairing. All four of these rise simultaneously when acting as air brakes; as

Table 2 One-Eleven Dimensions	Series 200, 300 and 400	Series 475	Series 500
Span	88ft 6in	93ft 6in	93ft 6in
Length overall	93ft 6in	93ft 6in	107ft 0in
Length of fuselage	83ft 10in	83ft 10in	97ft 4in
Height	24ft 6in	24ft 6in	24ft 6in
Wing area (gross)	1,003sq ft	1,031sq ft	1,031sq ft
Aspect ratio	8.0	8.5	8.5
Max internal cabin width	10ft 4in	10ft 4in	10ft 4in
Max internal cabin height	6ft 6in	6ft 6in	6ft 6in
Forward freight hold capacity	354cu ft	354cu ft	516cu ft
Rear freight hold capacity	180cu ft	180cu ft	260cu ft

spoilers, two on one side move upwards with the uprising aileron that causes the wing to drop, the two on the other side remaining stationary. The One-Eleven 400, 475 and 500 also have hydraulically-actuated lift dumpers inboard of the spoilers; these were fitted to meet US airline requirements, and the Series 300 has structural provision for them. The cantilever tail unit has a variable-incidence tailplane at the top of the fin, with a bullet fairing over the tailplane junction and variable-incidence mechanism. The fin is integral with the rear fuselage, and elevators and rudder are hydraulically-actuated. De-icing for the fin and tailplane leading edges is by engine bleed air tapped from the Spey compressors.

The circular-section fuselage is built up on continuous frames and stringers, and the maximum internal width of 10ft 4in at seat armrest height is 4½in wider than the Viscount at its widest; maximum internal cabin height is 6ft 6in. There are 24 VC10-type elliptical cabin windows on each side, measuring 14in deep×9¼in wide, and the maximum cabin pressure differential is 7.5lb/sq in. The hydraulically-operated ventral airstairs folding up into the rear fuselage are the first of their kind to be featured on a British airliner, and are reached through an inward-opening door for passengers in the rear pressure bulkhead. The forward passenger door in the port side has an optional power-operated airstair, and the floor sill height both for this door and the ventral entrance is 7ft 0in. There is a galley service door forward in the starboard side, and the galley units are normally at the front of the cabin to starboard on each side of this door. There are two under-floor baggage and

Above right:
Typical view of a One-Eleven interior with five-abreast seating.

Right:
The prototype takes off on her successful 27min maiden flight on the evening of Tuesday 20 August 1963.

freight holds, each with a door on the starboard side; the forward hold has a volume of 364cu ft and the rear hold, aft of the wings, has a volume of 180cu ft (156cu ft in the One-Eleven 475). For the long-fuselage Series 500 these holds were increased in volume to a total of 776cu ft, the forward one being 516cu ft and the rear one 260cu ft. Cabin length (excluding the flight deck) is 56ft 10in, this being increased to 70ft 4in on the longer Series 500. Air conditioning and pressurisation systems are fully duplicated with main components by Normalair-Garrett.

An Instant Aeroplane

One of several special features designed into the One-Eleven to enable rapid turn-round times to be achieved was the AiResearch Model GTCP85-115 gas turbine auxiliary power unit in the tail cone to provide ground electrical power, air conditioning on the ground and power for engine starting, without the use of special ground vehicles. Developed by AiResearch at its Phoenix, Arizona plant this APU provides both shaft and pneumatic power, and is run during take-off to avoid bleeding the engine air for cabin air conditioning. Shaft power, up to 200hp from the turbine, drives an alternator to provide AC electricity when the main engines are shut off, while compressed air is used to power air conditioning and heating systems on the ground and to start the Speys through Plessey air turbine constant speed drive starters.

The first production AiResearch APU destined for the One-Eleven prototype underwent ground tests by BAC mounted in a Viscount rear fuselage modified to represent the ventral passenger entrance. Another feature designed to aid quick turn-rounds was the single pressure refuelling point in the fuselage starboard side just under the wing leading edge; there was also provision for gravity refuelling.

Single-point refuelling at up to 410gal/min, together with the AiResearch APU, the two airstairs, waist-high baggage loading doors and carry-on baggage racks in the cabin all combined greatly to reduce turn-round times. Mohawk Airlines, within a year of beginning One-Eleven operations on 15 July 1965, was able to turn them round in 10min at terminal points with a full load of 69 passengers, baggage and cargo, or in only 6min at intermediate stops with partial passenger loads. The airline was able to claim in 1966 that faster terminal turn-rounds meant that it could schedule three flights instead of no more than two provided previously with piston-engined types, with an

Table 3	One-Eleven Performance				
	Series 200	Series 300	Series 400	Series 475	Series 500
Max cruising speed	541mph at 21,000ft	541mph at 21,000ft	541mph at 21,000ft	541mph at 21,000ft	541mph at 21,000ft
Best economic cruising speed	461mph at 25,000ft	461mph at 25,000ft	461mph at 25,000ft	461mph at 25,000ft	461mph at 25,000ft
Still air range with max fuel, ISA, and reserves for 230 miles diversion and 45min holding	2,130 miles	2,420 miles	2,420 miles	2,300 miles	2,165 miles
Still air range with typical capacity payload, ISA & same reserves as above	875 miles	1,430 miles	1,430 miles	1,865 miles	1,705 miles
Rate of climb at sea level and 345mph EAS	2,500ft/min	2,580ft/min	2,580ft/min	2,480ft/min	2,280ft/min
Take-off run to 35ft at sea level and ISA	6,850ft	8,000ft	7,600ft	5,900ft	7,300ft
Landing distance at sea level, ISA and max landing weight	4,970ft	4,880ft	4,880ft	4,800ft	4,800ft
Stalling speed (take-off flap setting)	123.5mph	131mph	131mph	114mph	121mph

Performance figures are at the maximum take-off weight
ISA = International Standard Atmosphere
EAS = Equivalent Airspeed

obvious improvement in revenue earned. And American Airlines One-Eleven co-ordinator Bruce Jobson neatly summed it up as 'an instant aeroplane', explaining: 'It is operationally self-supporting . . . well built and well thought out.'

The flight deck is designed for two-crew operation by the pilot and co-pilot, with provision for a third crew member in a 'jump' seat, and there is space available for a supernumerary or check pilot in a fourth seat behind the pilot. Ecko E 190 or Bendix RDR 1E weather radar is fitted in the nose, and an autoflare system for lower weather minima was developed by BAC in conjunction with Elliot Bros (London) Ltd and Bendix Eclipse Pioneer Division, making the maximum use of VC10 autoflare and autoland development work. Category 2 lower weather minima flight trials began on 7 July 1966 with the One-Eleven 400 prototype G-ASYD, and on 8 November that year this made four landings at London Gatwick in runway visual ranges of 250m, 200m and 400m and with fog being encountered at a height of 250ft. This was worse than the Category 2 standards (100ft decision height and a quarter of a mile

runway visual range) to which the One-Eleven was certificated as a result of these tests.

As related earlier, the One-Eleven's passenger seating capacity went up to 69 when Rolls-Royce Speys were substituted for the BS.75 turbofans, and this had gone up to 79 by the time of the first flight. As the result of successive increases in design weights (the One-Eleven 200's maximum take-off weight rose from 73,500lb to 74,500lb and eventually 79,000lb, and payload from 14,000lb to 16,850lb and eventually 19,000lb), maximum passenger capacity eventually rose to 89 for all versions except the Series 500. A movable divider bulkhead in the cabin allowed any ratio of first-class to tourist or economy passengers to be carried, a typical two-class layout seating 16 first-class passengers four-abreast and 49 tourist-class five-abreast; in an all-tourist interior 74 could be seated at 34in pitch.

The Series 500 could seat a maximum of 97-119 passengers, depending on its maximum weight, and had two additional overwing emergency exits, making two on each side. There is space for passengers' coats on the port side of the cabin aft

Above:
Braniff's first One-Eleven 203AE, N1541, seen in the final assembly stages at Hurn.

of the flight deck and, on the Series 200 and 300, in the rest vestibule. There are two toilets, one at the front of the cabin to port and the other at the rear to starboard or, in the Series 400 and 500, one each side of the cabin at the rear. A standard cabin interior was devised by the furnishing group of Vickers-Armstrongs (Aircraft) and the well-known US firm of Charles Butler Associates, which had also created interiors for a number of well-known US types, such as the Lockheed Super Constellation. This interior was offered as a standard one to One-Eleven customers to keep the aircraft's price down, and the airline could exercise its own choice of decor in such matters as seat upholstery and curtaining materials. By mid-1963 the One-Eleven's basic price was about £875,000 excluding seats.

For the One-Eleven 200 fuel capacity totals 2,235lmp gal in two integral wing tanks each formed by the wing torsion box; there is also an optional centre-section tank (which becomes a standard feature of the Series 300 and later versions) of 850lmp gal, giving a total capacity of 3,085lmp gal. Optional fuel tanks of 350lmp gal and

700lmp gal can be fitted, for example when the aircraft is used in the executive role. As mentioned previously, single point pressure refuelling is featured and, to meet US requirements, there was originally provision for fuel dumping, this being optional on the Series 200 and 300 and standard on the Series 400. But when, in mid-1964, the latter variant's maximum landing weight went up from 69,000lb to 76,000lb (the maximum take-off weight remaining the same at 78,500lb) there was no longer a need to provide for fuel dumping which FAA requirements demanded only if the difference between take-off and landing weights was over 5%: this no longer applied at the Series 400's higher landing weight.

The hydraulically-retracted undercarriage has twin wheels on each unit, the nosewheel retracting forward and the main wheels inwards into wheel bays in the fuselage centre-section. Dunlop wheels, tubeless tyres and four-plate heavy duty hydraulic disc brakes are featured, the Series 475 and 500 having similar but more powerful five-plate hydraulic disc brakes. The One-Eleven 200 and 300 have Dunlop Maxaret anti-skid units in the main wheels, and the Series 400, 475 and 500 have Hydro-Aire Hytrol Mk III anti-skid units.

The One-Eleven 200 is powered by two 10,410lb st (maximum take-off) RB.163-2 Spey 506-14 turbofans; the RB.163-2W Spey 506-14W with water injection for use in 'hot and high' conditions could also be fitted and was specified by British United Airways – chiefly for its West African route – and one or two other operators. Each Spey is suspended in its pod by a pair of steel beams built out from the rear fuselage, and each engine can be removed by a winch gear attached to the rear fuselage over the cowling. Thrust reversers are fitted, these consisting of internal clamshell doors that normally lie along the jet pipe wall, covering the reverser jet cascade apertures in the top and bottom of the jet pipe. When reverse thrust is selected, these doors swing rearwards and inwards to close the jet pipe and deflect the jet efflux through the cascade apertures, which are positioned so that neither the hot exhaust efflux nor stones from the runway are re-ingested into the engine.

It is interesting to recall that the One-Eleven was also considered with American engines in case a US airline wanted to order the type thus powered. Pratt & Whitney proposed a derated JT8D for the One-Eleven, as this turbofan powered the Boeing 727, and Pratt & Whitney's JTF10A-6 turbofan, an earlier version of which powered the projected Douglas DC-9 in its original four-jet form, was also studied for the One-Eleven. But studies of these powerplants in the end confirmed the view that the Spey was the best engine, and when American Airlines (probably the best potential customer for a US-powered version) ordered the One-Eleven 401, it was with Speys.

The One-Eleven 200AB prototype G-ASHG was rolled out at Hurn in British United Airways markings on Sunday 28 July 1963 for pressurisation and system checks, the first ground engine runs following two days later. After a final inspection programme, the day of the first flight arrived on Tuesday 20 August when, after weighing was completed, the aircraft was handed over to chief test pilot Jock Bryce, with Lt Cdr J. M. 'Mike' Lithgow as co-pilot. The first of several taxi runs was made at 13.30hrs and, after 2½hr had been spent examining and changing a brake unit, G-ASHG was refuelled for flight at 19.00hrs. She took off 42min later for a successful 27min first flight after a day of thunderstorms, and reached a height of 8,000ft and a speed of 220mph, the undercarriage and flaps being deliberately left down. The take-off weight was 58,683lb, including some 6,000lb of test instrumentation, and take-off distance was 3,150ft. Jock Bryce expressed satisfaction with the flight, describing the ailerons as 'impressively powerful' and Spey engine response as 'excellent'. There were now 60 One-Elevens on order, and the type seemed set for a bright future.

Below:
The prototype One-Eleven 200AB, G-ASHG, in BUA livery. The wing boundary layer fences are further outboard than on production aircraft; note the tail bumper on the ventral air-stairs door.

The Deep Stall Problem

By May 1963 three basic versions of the One-Eleven were on offer to the airlines. The One-Eleven 200 was the initial production version, cruising at some 200mph faster than the Viscount that it was intended to replace, and with the same fuel consumption as the Viscount 810, being intended chiefly for short and medium ranges from 200 miles upwards. Detail design of the One-Eleven 300 and 400 had started in November 1962, the Series 300 being dimensionally similar to the Series 200 but intended to carry a higher payload over a longer range; it had as standard the centre-section tankage that was optional on the Series 200. Heavier wing skin panels and shear webs and a strengthened undercarriage were featured to cater for a higher all-up weight, which was initially 82,000lb.

The Series 300 and 400 also had more powerful RB.163-25 Spey 511-14 turbofans of 11,400lb st take-off thrust in 4in longer nacelles. The Spey-25, as this variant was also known, differed from the Spey 506-14 in the Series 200 in having a five-stage low-pressure compressor instead of a four-stage one, and a higher pressure ratio of 20:1 instead of 16.8:1 in the Mk 506-14 (pressure ratio is akin to compression ratio in a piston engine). The Spey 510-14 of 11,000lb st, a derated version of the Mk 511-14, could also be fitted to both the Series 300 and 400 but in the event, American Airlines was the only operator to use the derated Spey 510-14, these engines in its One-Eleven 401s later being modified to Mk 511-14 standard. The latter variant with a water injection system fitted for 'hot and high' conditions became the Spey 511-14W and was specified by several operators, while a variant of the more powerful Spey 512-14DW in the One-Eleven 500 and 475 was later made available to Series 300 and 400 operators as the Spey 512-14 of 12,000lb st (maximum take-off).

The One-Eleven 400 was very similar to the Series 300 with the same strengthened wing and undercarriage, uprated Speys and the same centre-section tankage, but with a number of features added to meet US airline and airworthiness requirements. These included hydraulically-operated lift dumpers inboard of the wing spoilers to achieve shorter field lengths, emergency drop-out oxygen systems and – originally – provision for fuel dumping as mentioned previously. The maximum take-off weight was at first restricted to 78,500lb and then 79,000lb to be below the US legal limit of 80,000lb imposed for two-crew operation but, after this weight limit was lifted the Series 400 was certificated at a gross weight of 87,000lb.

The growth in thrust of the Spey since it was first chosen for the One-Eleven, combined with promising results of structural testing in static tests, enabled considerable improvements in design weights to be made, especially in the maximum landing weight and zero fuel weights. These were announced on 8 June 1964 by BAC and applied mainly to Series 300s and 400s for delivery in 1966 and later, the necessary minor structural changes to the landing gear and some other parts of the airframe being introduced on the production line. These weight increases are summarised in Table 4 below, and the zero fuel weight increase of 7,500lb for the Series 300 and 400 (this weight is usually the limiting case for the wing bending moment because the wings are empty of fuel and the fuselage is full with payload and crew) meant that these versions now had no weight limitations on payload, but only capacity ones.

Table 4
One-Eleven Weight Growth

	Max take-off wt (lb)	Max landing wt (lb)	Max zero fuel wt (lb)	Max payload (lb)
One-Eleven 200				
mid-1963	73,500	65,000	58,000	13,680
June 1964†	74,500	66,000	59,000	14,000
Jan 1965	76,500	67,500	62,500	16,850
1969	78,500	69,000	64,000	17,595
One-Eleven 300				
mid-1963	82,000	69,000	61,500	15,800
June 1964†	85,000	76,000	69,000	19,200
1969	87,000	78,000	71,000	22,278
One-Eleven 400				
mid-1963	78,500	69,000	61,500	15,400
June 1964†	78,500	76,000	69,000	19,200
1969	*87,000	78,000	71,000	21,413
One-Eleven 475				
current	92-98,500	84-87,000	73,000	21,527

† For aircraft ordered from June 1964 for delivery in 1966 or later.
* Max take-off wt is 92,000lb with new landing gear 'manacle beam'.

In other words, a 79-passenger Series 300 could carry a full passenger load with hand baggage (plus 5,340lb of freight and other baggage) over a distance of 1,194 miles with typical airline reserves; the original payload of 15,800lb could now be flown 1,700 miles with reserves, or 340 miles further than before, while the new capacity payload of 19,200lb could be flown a maximum of 1,194 miles. A succession of stages could now be flown without refuelling – a very important factor in local service-type operations; the Series 300 could now fly three successive sectors of 835, 345 and 445 miles with 74 passengers and baggage and full reserves without refuelling en route.

Increases in design weights were also possible for the One-Eleven 200 as a result of increased wing ultimate strength tests, and among the Series 200 weight increases announced on 25 January 1965 was a 20% increase in typical maximum payload from 14,000lb to 16,850lb. From the beginning of 1969 new Series 400s off the production line have incorporated a feature of the One-Eleven 500's undercarriage, the strengthened and improved 'manacle beam' that supports the main landing gear pintle. This has enabled maximum take-off weight to be increased by 5,000lb to 92,000lb.

Several military variants of the Series 200 and 300 were proposed in 1963 for the different roles of freight and vehicle carrying, VIP or personnel transport, casualty evacuation and as a radio operator or navigator trainer. For the latter roles, four training consoles could be fitted in the forward part of the cabin, each with a double instructor seat, while up to 49 soldiers could be carried in the normally empty rear part of the cabin without removing the training consoles. All these military variants could have featured a navigator's seat and console behind the two pilots; for VIP transport 28 passengers could be accommodated in first-class seats in the rear compartment and six in a forward compartment in luxury sleeperette seats around removable tables, while as a personnel transport either 52 or 73 passengers could be accommo-dated in airline-type seats. For casualty evacuation 12 stretcher cases and 34 sitting patients could be carried, plus two medical orderlies, and stretchers could be loaded via the ventral passenger steps. Late in 1966 BAC submitted preliminary proposals to the USAF for an aeromedical One-Eleven to meet the requirement eventually met by the C-9A Nightingale 'casevac' version of the DC-9 Series 32CF. BAC's One-Eleven submission could have carried 30 stretcher cases or 40 sitting patients for distances of over 2,000 nautical miles, and was powered by Spey-25s. Stretcher loading would have been through a large cargo door in the forward fuselage, similar to that in the One-Eleven 300 military freighter, but with a covered ramp to

Above:
This view shows the anti-spin parachute fairing under the tail cone of BUA's first One-Eleven, G-ASJA; this parachute was fitted after the prototype's deep stall crash. Note tail bumper on ventral air-stairs door.

protect patients from the weather and which would have folded into the aircraft.

This Series 300 freighter featured an upward-opening freight door forward in the port side measuring 6ft 1in×8ft 4in, and a strengthened floor that could take loads up to 75lb/sq ft over the whole floor area (measuring 44ft×9ft 6in), or up to 100lb/sq ft over its outer sections. The normal seat rails in the floor incorporated a 20in grid of freight lashing points capable of taking a 5,000lb load, and four standard 88in×108in freight pallets could be accommodated, with a pallet loading system. Small vehicles such as a Land Rover could also be carried, with load spreaders under the wheels. A mixed load of passengers and freight was also possible, separated by a rapidly movable bulkhead and, as a freighter, the Series 300 could take a load of 17,000lb over 1,070 nautical miles.

It was not until the end of 1974 that the first One-Eleven military freighter, one of three Series 475s for the Sultan of Oman's Air Force, was delivered; these had a slightly wider freight door measuring 10ft 0in×6ft 1in, and this door could have been fitted retrospectively to civil One-Eleven versions if so desired, although in the end no such civil freighter conversions were made. The only other military One-Eleven sales were two Series 217s to the Royal Australian Air Force as VIP transports, and two similar Series 423s for the Força Aerea Brasileira's Special Transport Group for use by the Brazilian President and other VIPs.

The Deep Stall Problem

Two One-Eleven static test airframes were also built, in addition to the BAC-owned prototype G-ASHG, which was to production standards. This completed its preliminary assessment on 13 September, 24 days after its first flight, in a programme of 19 flights totalling 30hr 30min. During this phase all the systems, both normal and emergency, functioned satisfactorily, asymmetric flying was done with single-engined landings and an engine cut on take-off, and flapless landings and take-offs were also made, while take-offs were carried out at weights of up to 73,000lb. By the third week in October the test programme had reached assessment of stability and handling characteristics during the approach to the stall, as well as the measurement of C_{Lmax} (maximum lift coefficient), and when G-ASHG took off from Wisley at 11.17am on the 22nd in perfect weather on its 53rd flight, piloted by Lt Cdr 'Mike' Lithgow with Capt R. 'Dickie' Rymer as co-pilot, a total of 42 approaches to the stall and recovery had been made satisfactorily in previous flights, which now totalled just over 80hr. These covered a range of flap angles from zero to full flap with the centre of gravity at between 0.16 SMC (standard mean chord) to 0.30 SMC, the former being the fully forward centre of gravity position and the latter an intermediate position.

On the 53rd flight four approaches to the stall with flaps up were made at 0.38 SMC (the cg fully aft) and it was on the fifth test at the same cg position with flaps lowered 8° that disaster struck when what later came to be known as a deep stall developed, from which it proved to be impossible to extricate the aircraft. It crashed just before noon in a field two miles from Chicklade, Wiltshire, striking the ground in an approximately horizontal attitude at a high vertical speed and low forward speed, only the tail unit, engines and port wing escaping destruction by impact and fire. All on board were killed; in addition to 'Mike' Lithgow and 'Dickie' Rymer the aircraft had been carrying R. A. F. Wright, senior flight test observer, G. R. Poulter, flight test observer and B. J. Prior, assistant chief aerodynamicist, all of Vickers-Armstrongs (Aircraft) Ltd, and two Hunting Aircraft men, C. J. Webb, the company's assistant chief designer, and D. J. Clark flight test observer. Their loss was a grievous blow; 'Mike' Lithgow, who was deputy chief test pilot, had set up a world speed record of 735.7mph in a Supermarine Swift at Tripoli, Libya, in 1953, as well as doing a great deal of the Attacker, Swift and Vanguard development flying, while Capt 'Dickie' Rymer had been the first airline pilot to fly the Viscount, in 1949, when he was a BEA captain, and he had also flown the world's first turbine-powered passenger carrying flight for BEA in the Viscount 630 prototype between Northolt and Paris on 29 July 1950.

The two flight recorders, one a 270-channel Royston Midas CMM24/7S/E in the tail and the other an eight-channel Colnbrook CID 02E in the fuselage, were both recovered from the wreckage, and it was these that enabled BAC to pinpoint and publish the cause of the accident so quickly, and to work out rapidly the modifications that would be necessary to prevent a recurrence. Without these 'black boxes' it might have taken months to find the true cause of the crash, during which time airline confidence and interest in the One-Eleven could have ebbed away and the whole programme might have been in serious jeopardy. Within a fortnight of the crash, on 4 November, BAC was able to issue a detailed statement on the cause of the accident based on analysing the flight recorder data, and this showed that during the fifth stall test the incidence had increased substantially above the figure anticipated. As the BAC statement describes it:

'The flight recorders show that the "g" break at the stall was large and abrupt, causing downward acceleration and further rapid increase of incidence. A condition rapidly developed in which it would be impossible for a pilot, even of Lithgow's calibre, to appreciate the situation soon enough and therefore prevent further build-up of incidence.

'As the incidence increased due to downward acceleration, the elevator started to trail up. This trail up was arrested and partial down elevator applied some 3 seconds after the "g" break but the aircraft response, as would be expected under these conditions of low forward speed and aft cg, was too slow to stop further increase of incidence.

'Eventually the incidence increased to a value where the effectiveness of tailplane and elevator was reduced to a fraction of the normal value. At this incidence the elevator servo tab power was insufficient to stop the elevator from trailing up and it reached the UP stop in spite of a large push force on the control column.

'The aircraft continued to descend at a high rate of descent, the fuselage attitude being substantially horizontal, and hit the ground flat. The aircraft did not spin and there is no evidence of structural or mechanical failure.

'The flight recorder data indicates that the engines were running and were used during the attempt to recover from the stall. The wreckage indicates that the engines were still revolving when the aircraft struck the ground and no evidence has been found which would indicate any in-flight malfunction.'

In this statement, prepared in consultation with the Chief Inspector of Accidents at the Ministry of Aviation, Group Captain J. B. Veale, who was conducting the enquiry into the crash, BAC revealed the main modifications it was making to the One-Eleven to prevent a similar accident happening again. The most important of these were a new revised and extended inboard wing leading edge profile to give a better nose-down pitching moment at the stall, and hence better stall recovery characteristics, and modifications were made to the elevator linkage to permit a more direct mechanical connection between the pilot's control and the elevator. A stick-pusher was fitted to prevent excessively nose-high angles of incidence being reached, and the wing fences were moved inwards. The testing of these modifications did delay certification by some months, but the deep stall investigation provided some valuable data in due course for other airliner manufacturers, especially Douglas with the DC-9, to whom BAC unselfishly provided information on the lessons it had learnt on the deep stall problem. As a result the DC-9 was given a larger tailplane and a revised wing leading edge profile. Because BAC was careful to publicise as soon as possible both the cause of the crash and the modifications it planned, customer confidence in the One-Eleven was retained to an astonishing degree, to the point where, in February 1964, not quite four months after the prototype was lost, American Airlines announced a repeat order for 10 to add to its initial order for 15 One-Eleven 401s, and Braniff ordered two more One-Eleven 203s to add to the 12 for which it had already contracted.

The original certification programme was based on the use of three fully instrumented aircraft, the first for British United, G-ASJA, being scheduled for systems development flying. The second and third for BUA, G-ASJB and G-ASJC, were originally scheduled for performance and radio trials but in the revised programme worked out after the prototype was lost they were detailed for further handling evaluation. To minimise delay G-ASJA was kept to its original tasks, but the test instrumentation on all three was changed and augmented to make up for the loss of that in the prototype, and all three were fitted with an anti-spin parachute in a fairing under the tail cone. These changes delayed the first flight of G-ASJA, the first production One-Eleven 201 for BUA, from Hurn, until 19 December 1963; it was followed into the air by G-ASJB on 14 February 1964 and by G-ASJC on 1 April. During March G-ASJB was fitted with the revised wing leading edge (at first in wooden form), as was G-ASJC, but on the 18th of that month, while being flown by a BAC pilot on a training flight who was making his first One-Eleven landing, G-ASJB made a heavy landing at Wisley and was considerably damaged when the undercarriage collapsed; the two BAC pilots, Mr S. Harris in the left-hand seat and Mr C. Moore, who was being checked out on the type, were uninjured. Some progress was made in rebuilding G-ASJB and it was allotted the new registration G-ASVT, but this was not completed and in its place BUA acquired another Series 201 registered G-ASTJ. G-ASJA made the first development flights outside the UK when it flew to Zurich on 2 March and visited Rome on 17-18 March.

The first Braniff One-Eleven 203, N1541, was rolled out at Hurn on 24 May and this made its first flight on 9 June. The fifth for BUA, G-ASJE, first flew on 5 May; this was the first fully-furnished one and was used for systems testing, including that of the radio, cabin air conditioning and furnishing. It was followed into the air by BUA's fourth, G-ASJD, on 6 July, but on 21 August this suffered minor damage in a wheels-up landing in open country near Boscombe Down, the tail parachute being streamed; the pilot had received from his instruments what subsequent examination of flight

recorder data clearly showed to have been a false impression of impending trouble. In fact there had been no malfunction of the aircraft or engines and G-ASJD was immediately repaired, soon taking its place again as one of six One-Eleven (five for BUA and Braniff's first) engaged in the certification programme. G-ASJC had flown to Madrid on 21 May for performance trials under 'hot and high' conditions, and G-ASJA left for Jan Smuts airport, Johannesburg on 16 January 1965 for five weeks of similar trials, having performed earlier trials of this kind at Dakar and Torrejon, near Madrid, the previous October and November. Low-speed handling trials were resumed during August 1964 with G-ASJC, the first One-Eleven to have the fully-powered elevator that replaced the original elevator design with servo tab control. As well as testing on the actual aircraft, development of these modifications involved, besides wind tunnel work, the use of 1/10th scale free-flight models dropped from helicopters at 3,000ft, analogue and digital computers and a flight simulator. During 21-31 August, G-ASJE made a demonstration tour of the Middle East, visiting Egypt, Saudi Arabia, Bahrain, Kuwait, Syria and the Lebanon, and in September G-ASJF made a similar tour of Germany.

The 11th One-Eleven to fly, G-ASJG for BUA, was the acceptance aeroplane for Air Registration Board certification flights; in addition to the new wing leading edge and revised elevator (now fully powered, with a new configuration of trim tabs), it also featured a longer and more pointed nose radome – which was to become standard – and an extractor cowl over the APU exhaust in the extreme tail. The One-Eleven 200 series was awarded its full unrestricted passenger transport category CofA on the ARB's recommendation on 6 April 1965, the first aircraft being delivered to BUA on that date, and this was followed by FAA (Federal Aviation Agency) Type Approval on 16 April. The way was now clear for airline services to begin; on 14 February BUA One-Eleven G-ASJI had completed a 200hr programme of route proving flights in Europe and the Mediterranean, in which 94 flights were made to 18 destinations over a period of 23 days, flight durations varying from 20min to 4½hr, and a daily utilisation of 8.7hr was achieved.

To make these flights fully representative of actual airline operations, no special ground preparations were made at any of the airports visited, routine and line maintenance was carried out wholly by BUA crews, and the majority of flights carried passengers with full cabin service provided. On 16 February G-ASJI left London Gatwick for similar route proving flights along BUA's West African route, calling at Lisbon, Las Palmas, Bathurst (Gambia), Freetown (Sierra Leone) and Accra (Ghana).

Above right:
An alternative mounting for the anti-spin parachute as seen on G-ASJD here was in a cylindrical canister supported by a mounting structure under the tail cone; this was fitted during deep stall flight testing.

Far left:
G-ASJA seen during the flight test programme with the anti-spin parachute in a fairing under the tail cone; this was also fitted to G-ASJB and G-ASJC and the test instrumentation in all three was changed and augmented.

Left:
Seen from a helicopter is G-ASJC, the first One-Eleven to have the fully-powered elevator that replaced the original elevator design as fitted on the prototype.

The One-Eleven 200 in Service

On 9 April 1965, after the 200hr programme of route proving flights in Europe and the Mediterranean, British United Airways inaugurated the world's first short-haul jet service, between London and Genoa, with One-Eleven 201 G-ASJJ flown by Capt S. G. Websper, BUA's One-Eleven fleet captain, with Capt D. N. Robinson as co-pilot and a cabin crew of four; there were some 25 booked passengers and 35 specially-invited guest passengers, including Mr Freddie Laker himself. They left Gatwick at 10.58hrs BST, touching down on Genoa's waterfront runway at 13.02hrs after a delay of 24min caused by a traffic hold over the destination, taking just over 2hr instead of the 1hr 40min scheduled for the 680-mile journey.

BUA One-Elevens accommodated 69-74 passengers in seats made by Aviation Traders (Engineering) Ltd, and the Charles Butler-styled cabin decor was in cream, light grey and pale blue colours to give a sense of real spaciousness. BUA's aircraft also had the optional centre-section tankage and Spey 506-14W engines with water injection.

BUA's scheduled passenger traffic increased by 49% in its first summer of One-Eleven operations, compared with 1964's established Viscount services, and at the end of seven months after starting jet services BUA One-Elevens were serving 38 destinations in Europe and Africa. With the full fleet of 10 in use the first five months of 1966 showed a passenger traffic increase of 35% over all routes served by the jets compared with the same

period in 1965. On 4 January 1966 BUA inaugurated the first domestic jet schedules in the United Kingdom when it began 'Interjet' One-Eleven services from London Gatwick to Glasgow, Edinburgh and Belfast. They also served the Channel Islands, Amsterdam and Rotterdam, the pilgrim centre of Lourdes, Barcelona, Malaga and Majorca, Gibraltar, Lisbon, Genoa, Malta, Las Palmas in the Canaries, Bathurst (Gambia), Freetown (Sierra Leone) and Accra (Ghana). Many inclusive tour holiday charters for tour operators such as Horizon Holidays were also flown, and after nearly two years in service BUA was getting more One-Eleven charter work than it was able to accept. By the end of 1966 BUA was finding that people were constantly specifying One-Elevens for their flights, and many were prepared to fly at a less convenient time to travel in one – load factors had not dropped as the type's novelty value wore off.

Like Mohawk and Braniff in the States, BUA found that the One-Eleven's self-contained nature enabled turn-rounds to be made in 6-10min at scheduled stops such as Glasgow and Edinburgh; at Glasgow BUA One-Elevens achieved the quickest turn-rounds on the airport. Initially the Interjet services were twice-daily to Glasgow and Edinburgh and once-daily to Belfast, but these service frequencies were increased, especially after BUA's merger in November 1970 with Caledonian Airways (Prestwick) Ltd to form British Caledonian Airways Ltd. B.Cal, as it was known for short, retained the BUA One-Eleven 201s in service to

Right:
Passengers boarding G-ASJJ for BUA's inaugural One-Eleven short-haul jet service from London Gatwick to Genoa on 9 April 1965. At the head of the steps are Mr Freddie Laker and Lord Douglas of Kirtleside, the latter being there in his capacity as chairman of Horizon Holidays, one of BUA's leading tour operator customers.

Far right:
Braniff's first One-Eleven, N1541, seen as temporarily registered G-ASUF to fly the Minister of Aviation, Mr Julian Amery, and a party of Ministry officials, to a meeting on Concorde with the French at Sud's Melun Villaroche works on 6 July 1964.

supplement the Series 501s and 509s ordered later, and new Interjet services from Southampton and Newcastle to Glasgow were introduced as well as Moonjet no-reservation night economy flights to Edinburgh. By 1973 the One-Eleven 201s were also linking Glasgow and Newcastle directly to Amsterdam, as well as flying London Gatwick to Paris Le Bourget services and operating the Gatwick-Le Touquet portion of the London-Paris 'Silver Arrow' rail/air/rail service.

From late 1976 all 16 B.Cal One-Elevens were withdrawn progressively for refitting with a restyled 'wide body' cabin interior, having more comfortable seats with reshaped seat backs and cushions, and up to an inch more leg room per seat row. New cabin sidewall panels and overhead enclosed hatrack/case and coat lockers were featured, and the complete refurbishing programme, costing about £600,000, was carried out by B.Cal at its Gatwick engineering base, using refurbishing kits supplied by BAC. B.Cal was the first One-Eleven operator to refit its fleet with 'wide body' interiors, and the first One-Eleven so modified went into service on domestic routes in February 1977.

Braniff's first One-Eleven 203 to be delivered, N1543, was the third it had on order. It was flown out on 11-13 March 1965 from Hurn to the airline's base at New York's Newark airport over the same 4,300-mile North Atlantic ferry route, via Prestwick, Keflavik (Iceland), Sondestrom (Greenland), Goose Bay (Labrador) and Montreal, that had been flown by the 147 Viscounts delivered to North America; many of the One-Elevens for other North American operators later followed this route. N1543 was flown to Dallas, Braniff's main base and headquarters, on the day of its arrival at Newark, and it embarked on an intensive programme of crew conversion training. On 25 April 1965 Braniff inaugurated the first truly short-haul jet services in the USA with the One-Eleven over a multi-stop route from Corpus Christi (Texas) to the twin cities of Minneapolis/St Paul (Minnesota) via six other places in Texas, St Louis (Missouri), Kansas City (Kansas) and Des Moines (Iowa). Braniff promoted the One-Eleven as the 'Fastback jet', and they were fitted out to seat 24 first-class and 39 coach-class passengers; they also had provision for fuel dumping, as did the other Series 200s for US customers. Braniff had announced on 30 September 1964 that it was taking an option on 12 more One-Eleven 203s for delivery in 1966, to add to the 14 it already had on order, but in the end this option was not taken up, not least because the airline decided to standardise on the Boeing 727 for its domestic jet schedules.

Braniff's One-Eleven load factor for May 1965, the first full month of operations, was 72%, compared with its June break-even load factor of 48.7% with three aircraft in service, and less than 40% with all 14 delivered. The airline was soon able to claim that it had never introduced a new aircraft which had received greater or faster public acceptance. From 18 towns and cities in June 1965 Braniff's One-Eleven network had grown after a year to serve 28 places in 13 states from Brownsville, Texas, on the Mexican border to Minneapolis/St Paul in the north, and to Washington DC, to Chicago and as far west as Lubbock and Amarillo in Texas. The shortest One-Eleven route sector, from San Antonio to Austin in Texas, was only 67 miles long, and there were several more of 140 to 150 miles, the longest being the 1,189 miles from Dallas to Washington DC. Braniff was getting a daily utilisation of 7.6hr from its three One-Elevens in early June 1965, and a year later, with all 14 in service, this had increased to 9hr 46min daily, and each aircraft was flying 14 airline sectors per day, the average sector length being 279 miles.

The One-Eleven's self-contained design features – in particular the tail-mounted APU, the ventral and forward airstairs, waist high baggage loading for the under-floor holds and single-point pressure

refuelling – enabled it to achieve a level of productivity in short-haul operations that was unrivalled up to that time, as is shown by the average of 3,960 landings achieved by each of the first seven One-Elevens delivered to the USA (five to Braniff and two to Mohawk) in its first 365 days of operation. Braniff's first to be delivered, N1543, made 4,040 landings, or an average of 11.5 a day in its first year of operations, flying 2,780hr or an average of 7.6hr daily. Braniff's fourth, N1545, delivered on 12 May 1965, made 4,080 landings, or 11.4 a day, in its first year, flying 3,020hr or 8.3hr a day; the three others, N1544, N1542 and N1546, managed an average of 10.3, 10.4 and 10.6 landings a day respectively, flying from 7.9 to 8.2hr daily. The first two for Mohawk, N2111J delivered on 15 May 1965 and N1112J delivered on 6 June, did just as well, if not better considering the more multi-stop and short-haul nature of Mohawk's One-Eleven network, with an average sector distance of about 172 miles. N2111J had 3,986 landings, or 11.8 a day, in its first year's service and N1112J made 4,190, or 10.5 a day; average daily utilisation, at 6.5hr for N2111J and 6.8hr for N1112J, was less than Braniff's because of the more short-haul nature of Mohawk's routes.

This ability to stand up to the hard pounding of intensive short-haul operations with the absolute minimum of technical 'snags', day in and day out, was deserving of the highest praise, and showed that a British aircraft could rival the best American competition in this respect; the One-Eleven's careful design for reliability and ease of maintenance had obviously paid off here. In the first two years of operations, Braniff's One-Eleven maintenance costs per flying hour had consistently been $20/hr or more below the original estimates made when the type was first ordered in 1961. By 1968 Braniff's first, N1543, had totalled 12,284 landings in three years of service, or an average of 11.2 a day, while Mohawk One-Elevens were

making 13 revenue flights in a typical day. The company's first, N2111J had made 16,834 flights, or 11.5 a day, in its first four years of service, and had flown 9,886hr. By 1977, after 12 years in service, it had logged about 45,000 flights, or a sustained average of 11 flights daily over this period.

Powerplant reliability is also vital in intensive short-haul operations, and in this respect the Spey 506-14 proved to be outstanding; in the 12 months following September 1966, the FAA authorised Time Between Overhaul for the Speys of Braniff's One-Elevens to increase from 3,000hr to 5,000hr. By 1969 there were 20 One-Elevens in the USA that had made over 15,000 landings, and a further 31 had logged over 10,000 each in four years of service. As Mr Murray P. White, president of BAC (USA) Inc, pointed out after stating these figures, 'Before the coming of the short-haul jet it was just not possible to get 11 or more useful revenue flights per day out of each aircraft. The block speeds were too low and the turn-round times too long.'

The first One-Eleven 204 for Mohawk Airlines Inc, N2111J, left Hurn on delivery through Prestwick on 15 May and was followed by its second, N1112J, on 6 June; N2111J was named *Ohio* by the airline's president, Mr Robert E. Peach, at a ceremony at Westchester County Airport, New York, shortly after its arrival. In its first three weeks it flew 100hr, with a daily utilisation of about 7hr, on pilot training and route proving. Mohawk started scheduled One-Eleven services officially on 15 July over a network serving nine cities in the northeastern USA between Cleveland (Ohio) and New York, and including Binghampton, Elmira/Corning, Buffalo, Rochester, Syracuse, Utica and White Plains in New York state; some ad hoc passenger services had already begun on 27 June. Mohawk was the first airline to operate One-Elevens over an exclusively short-haul network, with one route

(Utica-Syracuse) only 47 miles in length, and the longest, from Utica to Cleveland, was 349 miles.

Mohawk One-Elevens seated 69 passengers in a one-class Charles Butler-styled interior that was unusual in having the Aerotherm Zephyr II seats in alternate four and five-abreast rows; turn-round times were further shortened by having carry-on baggage racks at the front and rear of the cabin. Token cabin dividers, little higher than the seat backs, were also featured at either end of a central conference area, and these also helped to speed embarking and disembarking, since passengers who entered by the forward door seldom went aft of the forward divider, and the same applied to those who boarded by the ventral airstairs. To speed up baggage hold and freight handling,

Mohawk replaced the standard webbing in the holds with thicker, heavier material with which the forward hold was divided into three sections, this enabling the freight to be split up, as it was loaded, by destination. This attention to detail paid off, because Mohawk was able to achieve scheduled turn round times of 6min maximum with the One-Elevens at intermediate stops, compared to the 8min of its piston-engined Convairs, and 10min at terminal stops as compared to the 15min achieved with Convairs. These faster terminal turn-rounds could mean that Mohawk was able to schedule three flights where previously it could provide no more than two.

By the beginning of 1966 Mohawk was able to report that traffic had increased 35% with the

One-Eleven on a comparable time of day basis with the Convair 240s operated previously; the One-Elevens had brought first-ever jet service to 14 of the 34 airports served; these included New York's Newark and La Guardia as well as Kennedy International. Direct operating costs per seat-mile averaged only 1.83 cents, compared with the 2.2 cents originally forecast and 2.3 cents for the Convairs. With five One-Elevens in service by early 1966, Mohawk was flying 30% of its system seat-miles daily with these jets, with its 27 Convairs flying the remaining 70%; the One-Eleven route network now covered 16 towns and cities. Mohawk found that the One-Eleven's productivity, because of the additional seat-miles and schedules it made possible by virtue of its shorter time on the ground and faster block speeds, was more than double that of each piston-engined aircraft it replaced.

Mohawk had announced its initial order for four One-Eleven 204s on 24 July 1962, and eventually operated a fleet of 21 of the type. In view of this, it is not a little ironical to recall that the original order was viewed by the Civil Aeronautics Board with some misgivings, and that in December 1962 CAB chairman Alan Boyd wrote to Mohawk's president warning him of the 'substantial financial risk' of buying One-Elevens, which the CAB considered to be too large. In his letter Mr Boyd expressed concern that Mohawk's load factor before it acquired modern equipment (ie Convairs) was 58% whereas currently it was only 48%, although revenue passenger-miles had increased by about 400%. Mr Boyd warned that if One-Elevens were ordered Mohawk would run the risk of losing its Federal subsidy for local service operations. 'We are impelled', he wrote, 'to specifically place the management of Mohawk on notice – as we have done in prior situations – that it is our intention that the Government will not, through subsidy payments, bear the burden of any worsening of Mohawk's position . . .' Mohawk's president replied to this argument by asserting that his

One-Elevens would reduce the airline's need for subsidy, and since the Mohawk order was being financed privately, and not underwritten by the US Government, it went ahead and in the event the CAB's misgivings proved to be unfounded. Mohawk ordered a fifth One-Eleven on 31 March 1964 and took up options on two more on 19 February 1965; a further two on option were taken up a year later and a third option (making 10 in all) on 4 May 1966. Orders for a further eight were placed during 1967-69, and Mohawk also acquired the three One-Eleven 215s of Aloha Airlines Inc when that operator went over to Boeing 737s. The last airline Series 200 to be built was Mohawk's

One-Eleven Arrives at the Ramp

Ground markers are placed at the wing tips. Only baggage/cargo trucks are allowed inside the arc subtended between the nose and tail on the right-hand side of the aircraft. These trucks are positioned three paces from the cargo door sills.

Single point refuelling coupling connected. Preset fuelling at 363 US gallons (1,090kg) per minute.

New passengers board and baggage/cargo loading begins.

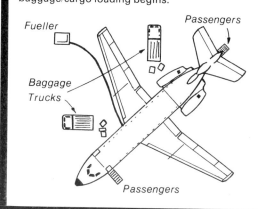

Fueller

Passengers

Baggage Trucks

Passengers

N1129J, which left Hurn on delivery on 17 May 1969 as the first One-Eleven 510s for BEA were coming off the line.

In 1971 a merger was decided on in principle between Mohawk Airlines and Allegheny Airlines Inc of Washington National Airport, the much bigger local service (or regional) airline that was then serving over 100 towns and cities in 17 states in the northeastern USA, as well as Ontario in Canada. Allegheny had previously merged, on 1 July 1968, with Lake Central Airlines Inc of Indianopolis, which had operated a network stretching from Baltimore and Washington DC, largely through Ohio, Michigan and Indiana; Lake

Central had become the first US operator of the Nord 262 turboprop in May 1965. Also in May 1965 Allegheny had put its first Allison 501-powered Convair 580 into service, and eventually operated over 40 until the last was withdrawn in June 1978; it had previously operated five Napier Eland-powered Convair 540s, between 1959 and 1962.

Allegheny's first jet, a leased DC-9 Series 31, entered service in July 1966, and the airline had 31 examples of this variant by the time the necessary CAB and shareholders' approval for the merger with Mohawk was given early in 1972. The merger became effective on 12 April that year, and in anticipation of these approvals and the merger

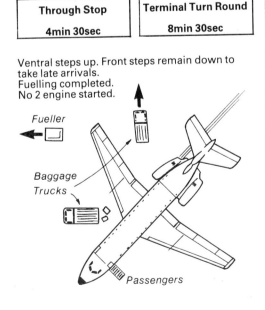

Through Stop	Terminal Turn Round
4min 30sec	8min 30sec

Ventral steps up. Front steps remain down to take late arrivals.
Fuelling completed.
No 2 engine started.

Fueller

Baggage Trucks

Passengers

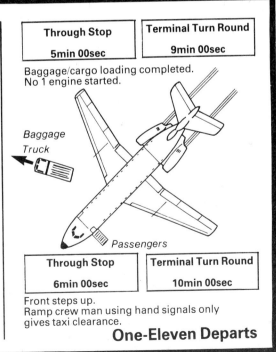

Through Stop	Terminal Turn Round
5min 00sec	9min 00sec

Baggage/cargo loading completed.
No 1 engine started.

Baggage Truck

Passengers

Through Stop	Terminal Turn Round
6min 00sec	10min 00sec

Front steps up.
Ramp crew man using hand signals only gives taxi clearance.

One-Eleven Departs

taking effect Braniff had sold eight of its One-Eleven 203s to Allegheny, plus three more already leased to it, shortly before; Braniff was then in the process of building up its Boeing 727 fleet, and its One-Elevens were now surplus. With Mohawk's own One-Eleven 204s integrated into its fleet, Allegheny now had 31 of the type in service, together with the DC-9s and 17 ex-Mohawk Fairchild FH-227B turboprops, which were soon sold off. The One-Elevens continued in service with Allegheny, which changed its name to US Air Inc on 26 October 1979, and by 1983 some of these jets had exceeded 65,000 landings, averaging 42min per flight and 10-11 flights daily.

Another local service carrier, Bonanza Air Lines Inc of Las Vegas, which operated about 2,400 miles of routes in Nevada, Arizona, Utah and California, and which had ordered three One-Eleven 206s in October 1962, was not so lucky as Mohawk in getting the aircraft of its initial choice. In March 1963 the CAB refused it, by a three-to-two majority vote, a US Government-guaranteed loan to buy the One-Elevens on the grounds that it thought the airline's traffic forecasting was too optimistic and the British jet was too large. While Bonanza's net earnings in 1962 had quadrupled to $400,000, its built-in Federal subsidy remained constant at $3.3million, and its purchase of a fleet of eight Fairchild F-27A turboprops had been underwritten by the US Government to the tune of $5.4million; under the terms of this loan the CAB had to give its approval of any future orders. Bonanza's One-Eleven order, unlike Mohawk's, was not financed privately and so in this respect it had no choice but to bow to the CAB's opinion; in fairness to the CAB it would have taken the same decision if a US-designed airliner had been involved. But on 11 July 1963 Bonanza announced an order for three Douglas DC-9s, later giving as its reasons the

DC-9's somewhat greater payload capacity, the better product support to be expected from an aircraft built in Los Angeles, coupled with the name of Douglas, which was much better known in the States to the travelling public than BAC's. Bonanza's first DC-9 Series 10 was delivered in December 1965 and in 1968 the airline became part of Air West Inc (later Hughes Airwest Inc).

The next European operator after BUA to put the type into service was Aer Lingus, which began One-Eleven 208 services over the Dublin-Cork-Paris route on 3 June 1965 with EI-ANE *St Mel*, the first of four delivered. This had been preceded by a shakedown and demonstration tour in which in six days starting on 27 May the One-Eleven made 27 flights (including 13 demonstrations) and visited a dozen European cities on the Aer Lingus network. The Irish airline had placed its One-Eleven order on 3 May 1963, and had been studying various types of jet since 1959, but for some time jet competition from other airlines on European routes was seen as an effective bar to further expansion. The problem for Aer Lingus was not only the right type of jet but also judging accurately the correct moment for its introduction; the airline's frequencies on European routes were low and average sector distances were short because of the multi-stop nature of the routes. All these factors pointed to the One-Eleven, which was the right size to enable very attractive frequencies to be offered, and this was proved when Aer Lingus passenger traffic between Ireland and Europe increased by 19% in August and no less than 26% in October 1965. For April/May 1966 the Shamrock Jets, as they were promoted, produced a 33⅓% increase in passengers carried over the same period in 1965 on routes from Manchester (Aer Lingus' second traffic generating point). Passenger increases to Dusseldorf and Frankfurt were no less than 85% and 62% respectively. The Shamrock Jets accommodated 74 passengers and had provision for future all-weather landing capability built into them.

Aloha Airlines Inc of Honolulu, Hawaii ordered two One-Eleven 215s on 15 March 1965, and a third in October 1966, and these were put on to the inter-island routes linking Kauai, Honolulu, Maui and Hilo, the first service being flown on 27 April 1966. The first Aloha One-Eleven, N11181 *Queen Kapidani*, left Gatwick on delivery on 15 April, and when the second, N11182, flew into Honolulu just after dawn on 8 June on delivery eight days ahead of schedule, Aloha's president, Kenneth F. C. Char, flew out to meet it in his first One-Eleven, together with an Aloha Viscount 745 to provide a vantage point for newsmen and photographers. In its first month of operation, the first one made 404 landings, a rate of 13 a day, on trips averaging 24min, and this emphasised the really short-haul nature of Aloha's network, on which the longest

sector was only 250 miles and the shortest 100 miles. The two Alohajets, as they were called, seated 79 passengers and had both completed over 5,000 landings by the end of 1966 and achieved an average daily utilisation of 5hr over what Aloha claimed to be the shortest jet routes in the world; the delay rate of only 1.08% per 100 departures set a record low and by the end of 1966 direct operating costs, excluding depreciation, showed a 23% improvement over the original forecasts. And in July 1968 Aolha's first, N11181, completed its 10,000th landing in service just 803 days after it was delivered; its average technical delay rate over this period was below 1% and it was now making 12 25min flights daily as one of the three Alohajets.

During the airline's 20th birthday celebrations in October 1966 Aloha's president announced an order for a third One-Eleven 215 for delivery in June 1967 and options on a fourth for delivery in 1968 and a fifth in 1969, mentioning his management's confidence in the continuing

development of the type. Mr Kenneth Char also added 'the after sales service to Aloha over the last six years on Viscount and One-Eleven aircraft is unquestionably the finest service ever given Aloha by any manufacturer and was a major influence in Aloha's decision to re-order One-Elevens.' This was praise indeed, but to meet likely future traffic growth and the intense competition it faced from Hawaiian Airlines Inc on the inter-island routes, Aloha placed an initial order for two Boeing 737-200s early in 1968 instead of taking up options on a fourth and fifth One-Eleven. This was presumably because the Boeings could be delivered earlier than the long-fuselage One-Eleven 500 which Aloha would have needed to remain competitive.

Hawaiian Airlines itself had announced plans to order three One-Eleven 209s in January 1963 for delivery in 1965, but a contract was not signed because in July 1962 the CAB had ordered a sweeping investigation of both Hawaiian and

Inset left:
The two Central African One-Elevens entered service with Zambia Airways, the successor to CAAC, in December 1967, and served with it until 1975.

This spread:
Laker Airways One-Eleven 320Ls were used to pioneer the 'Time Charter' principle in inclusive tour holiday charters, and flew as much as 17 hours daily at the peak weekend period.

Inset Bottom:
One-Eleven 301 G-ATPL was leased by British Eagle in 1967 to SAS, which named it 'Arnold Viking'. Note the Norwegian, Danish and Swedish flags on the cowling.

Aloha with a view to reducing or eliminating uneconomic competition between them, and reducing their subsidy payments. Hawaiian's proposed One-Eleven order never received positive CAB approval, and the airline had a new president early in 1964, this change in management resulting in a change of mind to the Douglas DC-9, an order for two 90-passenger DC-9s being announced in November that year. Hawaiian began 'Royal Fan Jet' services with DC-9s on 1 April 1966, four weeks before the Alohajets.

In October 1962 two One-Eleven 207s were ordered by Central African Airways Corporation, which had been formed in 1946 by the governments of Northern and Southern Rhodesia and Nyasaland, and which had its main base in Salisbury. These two, VP-YXA and VP-YXB, were nearing completion when Mr Ian Smith made Rhodesia's fateful Unilateral Declaration of Independence on 11 November 1965 in Salisbury, putting white-ruled Rhodesia politically at odds with the neighbouring (now independent) black states of Zambia (formerly Northern Rhodesia) and Malawi (formerly Nyasaland), which had been its partners in the Federation of Rhodesia and Nyasaland during 1953-63. In these circumstances delivery of the two One-Elevens had to be deferred, as Rhodesia was now an 'illegal' regime and increasingly isolated politically, both by world opinion and by sanctions; the two were leased by the Zambian Government to British Eagle International Airways from May 1966 for a period of up to 18 months. They differed from other series 200s in having the more powerful Spey-25 Mk 511-14 engines of the Series 400 for 'hot and high' African conditions.

The first was delivered, still as VP-YXA, to London Heathrow on 22 April 1966 to emerge soon after in British Eagle livery as G-ATTP *Swift*, and VP-YXB, after being demonstrated at Heathrow in the Zambian registration 9J-RCI on 10 May, was delivered to British Eagle on 27 May, becoming G-ATVH. It was later leased to Swissair for 13 months from 1 April 1967 because of delays in the Swiss airline's DC-9 deliveries; it was used for scheduled services from Zurich to Dusseldorf, Prague and Nice. The other ex-CAAC One-Eleven, G-ATTP *Swift*, flew the first British Eagle jet service between London and Glasgow's Abbotsinch airport on 9 May 1966 after a proving flight over this route on the 2nd, as well as operating the other British Eagle routes. In December 1967 it became 9J-RCH and joined 9J-RCI in service with Zambia Airways Corporation, which had been formed on 1 September that year to take over from Zambia Airways, the CAAC subsidiary formed in 1963. Central African Airways itself survived UDI but had been rendered obsolete by political events; it ceased operations on the last day of 1967 following Zambia's ending of direct air services to Rhodesia as part of the sanctions policy. The new Zambia Airways Corporation used the One-Elevens on the more important domestic and regional routes from Lusaka, serving Blantyre (Malawi), Dar es Salaam (Tanzania), Nairobi (Kenya), and Mauritius in the Indian Ocean via a technical stop at Tananarive (Madagascar). Early in 1975 they were both sold by Zambia to Dan-Air Services Ltd and were delivered to London Gatwick on 29 March that year, becoming G-ATTP and G-ATVH again; the latter was named *City of Newcastle-upon-Tyne* by the Lord Mayor of that city on 28 October 1976.

Below:
Laker One-Eleven G-AVBY was leased to Air Congo immediately on delivery in May 1967, and flew that airline's trans-Africa route from Lagos in Nigeria to Nairobi, as well as domestic and regional routes from Kinshasa.

Table 5
One-Eleven Production

	No built	Reg'n	Date of Delivery
Series 200	58		
First delivery		G-ASJA	6/04/65
Last delivery		N503T	8/07/69
Series 300	9		
First delivery		G-ATPJ	8/06/66
Last delivery		G-AVYZ	11/04/68
Series 400	69		
First delivery		N5015	22/12/65
Last delivery		D-ANNO	22/12/70
Series 475	10		
First delivery		OB-R-953	26/07/71
Last delivery		YR-BCR	28/07/81
Series 500	85		
First delivery		G-AVMJ	29/08/68
Last delivery		YR-BCO	12/03/82
	231*		

* Includes three pattern aircraft for Rumania, but not Rumanian production. Excludes last two unsold Series 475s.

Below:
First executive One-Eleven was the Series 211 D-ABHH for the West German department store group Helmut Horten GmbH. This well-equipped One-Eleven was fitted for Category 2 landings and had a Doppler navigation system as well as Spey 506-14W jets with water injection.

Series 300 Customers
Kuwait Airways had ordered three One-Eleven 205s, plus one on option, featuring the optional centre-section tankage, on 9 August 1962 and later changed over to the Series 301 variant. These would have been delivered at about the same time as the airline's three DH Trident 1Es, the first of which was delivered on 20 March 1966 to add to the two Comet 4Cs already in service. The addition of a third type of jet to such a small fleet would have proved unnecessarily costly in such things as spares holdings, maintenance and crew training, and so after reflection Kuwait Airways decided to sell its One-Elevens before delivery to British Eagle International Airways, and to standardise on Tridents and later Boeing 707-369Cs as first-line equipment. The three One-Elevens, registered 9K-ACI, 9K-ACJ and 9K-ACK, became respectively G-ATPJ *Stalwart*, G-ATPK *Spur* and G-ATPL *Superb* with British Eagle, which took delivery of the first of these on 8 June 1966.

They were soon operating domestic routes from London to Glasgow and Liverpool, and internationally from London to Stuttgart, Rimini on the Italian Adriatic coast, Pisa, Luxembourg, Dinard and La Baule in Britanny, Perpignan, Palma in Majorca, and to Tunis and Djerba in Tunisia, most of these being charter and inclusive tour holiday destinations. G-ATPJ was leased to KLM for several months from 29 March 1968, and also to SAS, and G-ATPK was leased to Swissair for a time in 1968 and later, from March to October 1970, to Bahamas Airways Ltd as VP-BCP; G-ATPL was leased to SAS in 1967, which named it *Arnold Viking*, but it retained its British registration. Dan-Air Services later acquired both G-ATPJ and G-ATPL, taking delivery of them in March 1970 and 14 October 1969 respectively, while G-ATPK was sold to Laker Airways Ltd, being delivered on 18 February 1971.

British Eagle had also ordered two One-Eleven

Right:
**This view of an executive
One-Eleven interior shows the
working lounge area with
airline-type seats in groups of four
with tables, and a settee.**

304s on its own account and these, G-ATPH *Salute*
and G-ATPI *Supreme*, were delivered on 28 April
and 25 May 1967 respectively. They operated
scheduled services and inclusive tour holiday
charters but after British Eagle went out of business
near the end of 1968 they were both sold in April
1969 as CF-QBN and CF-QBO to Quebecair Inc, a
small Canadian regional carrier that operated
services from Montreal to towns on both sides of
the St Lawrence river and its associated Gulf. The
two 74-passenger One-Elevens went straight into
service at the end of April, superseding Fairchild
F-27 turboprops on key routes, for on the 25th of
that month Quebecair had been granted an
emergency licence to operate the strike-bound Air
Canada's flights linking Montreal, Ottawa and
Toronto, providing 700 seats daily, in addition to its
own route commitments.

Services began the same day, with the
One-Elevens operating a total of 23 flights daily
plus a number of charters, and jet schedules soon
built up to 200 flights a week. These linked
Montreal and Quebec to Mont Joli on the Gaspe
peninsula, and to Saguenay, Baie Comeau, Sept
Iles and Wabush in southern Quebec. Passenger
acclaim for the One-Eleven was immediate, and not
just because it was introduced on to temporarily
strike-bound routes; the BAC jets proved their
ability to serve economically a relatively short-haul
network covering mainly sparsely settled areas of
population. Quebecair acquired a third One-Eleven
Series 402 CF-QBR, built for Philippine Air Lines as
PI-C1141 and leased to Bavaria Fluggesellschaft in
1967 as G-AVEJ; this left Hurn on delivery on 12
March 1973. Quebecair's three One-Elevens were
temporarily withdrawn from use at Montreal on 31

October 1981, but re-entered service late the
following April, and Series 204 N1117J was in
addition leased from US Air for several months
from May 1982. At the end of that year Quebecair
put into service two Series 420s, LV-IZR and LV-IZS,
acquired from the Argentine operator Austral;
these became C-GQBP and C-GQBV respectively,
and helped make up the loss of capacity caused by
Quebecair's lease of three Boeing 737-296s to Pan
American early in 1983 for its services from Berlin.

The two Series 304s were sold in 1984 to a new
Welsh charter airline Air Cymru, or Airways
International (Cymru) Ltd. The first, C-FQBN, was
delivered as G-YMRU on 22 March, followed in
November by C-FQBO which became G-WLAD.

Laker Airways Ltd, just formed by Mr Freddie
Laker after leaving BUA, announced an order for
three One-Eleven 320Ls on 8 February 1966 and
these, G-AVBW, G-AVBX and G-AVBY, were
delivered on 25 February, 8 April and 13 May 1967;
a fourth was later ordered and this, G-AVYZ,
followed on 11 April 1968. These were used to
pioneer the principle of 'Time Charter' in the
holiday charter business, in which the airline
virtually 'wet leased' an aircraft to a tour operator
for a 12-month period at a rate based on a
minimum of 1,700hr flying. For every hour flown
over this relatively modest figure the tour operator
got a rebate which brought the overall cost of his
flying down and enabled him to price any route as
he saw fit and to cross-subsidise his routes any
way he wished. If he wished to generate traffic
among those taking a second holiday he could,
with summer rebate hours in credit, get the overall
utilisation rate low in the winter and 'shoulder'
months.

Right:
This view shows the executive suite forward that can be used as a conference area, with bar facilities to the left.

'Time Charter' was used initially by Laker on behalf of two of Britain's leading package holiday firms, Wings and Lord Brothers; Laker later acquired a 75% holding in the latter and also took over Arrowsmith Holidays, a smaller Liverpool-based tour operator. In their first summer of operations, the 84-passenger One-Elevens G-AVBW and G-AVBX were flying 54 sectors (or about 56,000 miles) a week to 22 destinations in 12 countries, ranging from Greece and the Adriatic to Tunisia, and Tenerife in the Canary Islands. The third One-Eleven, G-AVBY, had been leased to Air Congo immediately on delivery, and started services from Kinshasa (formerly Leopoldville) on 15 May 1967. It took over from DC-6s Air Congo's trans-Africa route from Lagos (Nigeria) via Kinshasa to Bujumbura (Burundi), Entebbe (Uganda) and Nairobi. It also replaced DC-4s on routes to Ndola and Lusaka in Zambia, which were flown weekly, and flew five domestic flights weekly from Kinshasa to Lubumbashi.

Both in Africa and Europe the Laker aircraft were worked very hard, the Gatwick-based pair flying a peak 17hr per aircraft every Saturday during the first summer's operations on holiday charters, this rate falling to about 10hr by the following Tuesday, and both aircraft spent Wednesdays at Gatwick on preventive maintenance before working up to the weekend peak again. To meet exactly these holiday flight schedules, planned many months previously, put a high premium on reliability, and in this respect the One-Elevens proved to be outstanding. By August 1969, with four One-Elevens in service, peak weekend utilisation had fallen slightly to 14hr 45min, and 33 destinations in 11 countries in Europe and North Africa were being served, from

Gatwick, Liverpool, Manchester and Berlin. One aircraft operated from the latter city on behalf of the German tour operator Flug-Union, serving 10 holiday centres in five countries. The four One-Elevens were flying an average flight length of 1,010 miles in August 1969, for which the average flight time was 2hr 25min. In February 1971 Laker Airways acquired a fifth, the ex-British Eagle Series 301 G-ATPK, and after the airline's unfortunate demise early in 1982 the four One-Eleven 320Ls were leased by Laker's receiver to British Caledonian Airways and re-registered in April. G-AVBW, G-AVBX and G-AVBY became respectively G-BKAU, G-BKAV and G-BKAW, while G-AVYZ became G-BKAX. G-ATPK is now owned by Chemco Equipment Finance Ltd of London, WC2.

Executive and Resales

The One-Eleven also had obvious possibilities as an executive and VIP transport, and a few were built as such, although most used in this role were converted from second-hand airline One-Elevens. First executive One-Eleven to be built, and also the first Weybridge-built aircraft, was Series 211 D-ABHH delivered to the West German stores group Helmut Horten GmbH on 29 January 1966, replacing the Fokker F.27 Friendship 100 they had previously used, and fitted with Spey 506-14W jets with water injection. Based at Dusseldorf, D-ABHH was used to fly departmental chiefs between leading German cities and the head office. Two more bizjet One-Eleven 212s, N502T and N503T, were supplied to the Tennessee Gas Transmission Corp, or Tenneco Inc, of Houston, Texas, which also operated a pair of Viscount 700s; a few years ago Tenneco acquired Helmut Horten's D-ABHH,

which became N504T. N502T left Hurn on delivery on 5 April 1966 after having its executive interior installed by Marshalls Ltd at Cambridge, a BAC-appointed specialist contractor for One-Eleven executive conversions, as was Pacific General Manufacturing Inc of Burbank, California. Both Tenneco One-Elevens had a 500Imp gal long range tank, and have flown to Honolulu and South America as well as within the USA.

Long range tanks could be fitted to executive One-Elevens to give a range of up to 3,500 miles plus 2hr reserves, giving non-stop coast-to-coast capability across the USA, and a later customer option that became available was an inertial navigation system. Late in 1964 Page Airways International of Washington National Airport, and later of Rochester, New York state, had been appointed by BAC as exclusive distributor in the USA for executive One-Elevens, and had ordered two such Series 400s for delivery in the autumn of 1966 and spring 1967. The Royal Australian Air Force ordered two One-Eleven 217s in January 1966 for VIP transport and these, serialled A12-124 and A12-125, were delivered in January and February 1968 to No 34 (ST) Squadron at Fairbairn, Canberra, where, with several other types in the squadron, they shared the duty of flying Government ministers and other VIPs. Like those of Central African Airways, they had the uprated Spey-25 Mk 511-14 turbofans to cater for 'hot and high' conditions.

US corporate customers sometimes went outside the United States to acquire their One-Elevens, as when BUA sold its first production aircraft, G-ASJA, early in 1970 to E.T. Barwick Industries of Chamblee, Georgia as N734EB; this was first flown for its new owners, a firm of carpet manufacturers, at Cambridge on 7 March after executive refurbishing by Marshalls, whose Class B registration G-52-1 it bore for this flight, and it was delivered as N734EB on 2 April 1970. In 1976 it was

sold to Mexico as XB-MUO for use by that country's Olympic Committee (Comite Olimpico Mexicana); its civil registration was later cancelled and it bore the military serial TX-0201 in service with the Fuerza Aerea Mexicana, being used as a VIP transport from October 1976 by the Office of the Mexican President, and based at Mexico City with the Presidential VIP transport squadron. It later reverted to XB-MUO under the ownership of Mario Vasquez Rana, and in 1979 was sold to Omni International with the Cayman Island registration VR-CAQ, presumably for tax reasons; in 1980 it was sold by Omni Aircraft Sales to Kenny Rogers Ltd of Beverley Hills (Kenneth and Marianne Rogers) as N3756F, shortly afterwards, on 20 May becoming N97KR. In March 1984 it went to the Tracinda Corp, who have now traded it in for a DC-9.

BUA's fourth One-Eleven 201, G-ASJD, by now with British Caledonian and named *City of Edinburgh*, was sold to the Ministry of Defence (Aviation) in October 1971 for use by the Blind Landing Experimental Unit at Bedford; it was not delivered there until 26 March 1973, bearing the RAF serial XX105. It was used to investigate new radio and navaid equipment and technologies for Category 3 fully automatic landings, and the use of varying steep approach angles for noise reduction. For the latter task, a Direct Lift Control system was installed, and it was later used by the Flight

Systems Squadron at RAE Bedford; most of the cabin is taken up by display and control consoles, and analogue computer, digital recording equipment an inertial navigation system and other equipment, and there is seating for 12 passengers in the rear of the cabin.

By 1981 B.Cal still had seven of the ex-BUA One-Eleven 201s in service; an eighth, G-ASJJ, had been written off in BUA service on the evening of 14 January 1969 when it crashed soon after take-off from Milan's Linate Airport en route to London Gatwick; it had been diverted to Milan from Genoa on the outward flight. There was apparently a loss of power in both engines after a normal take-off, and G-ASJJ was force-landed on snow-covered sand about two miles from the end of Runway 18; there were no fatalities, but seven out of the 26 passengers and seven crew were injured, two of them seriously. G-ASJJ was replaced by Series 408 G-AWKJ acquired from Channel Airways.

In 1981 B.Cal sold the seven remaining One-Eleven 201s through Westair Holdings to its subsidiary Pacific Express Inc of Chico, California, which operated a network of commuter routes mostly within the state of California. The first, G-ASJC, was delivered as N101EX from Gatwick on 10 December 1981 and was followed by G-ASJE to G-ASJI, re-registered N102EX to N106EX, and G-ASTJ, now N107EX; the last to be delivered, N102EX, left Gatwick on 10 June 1982. All seven were initially registered to Security Pacific Commercial Leasing, and in addition Series 204 N1120J was acquired on lease from US Air, and Series 203 N1548 was leased from US Air, but both have now been returned. Pacific Express used its One-Elevens to serve Chico, Sacramento, San Francisco, the Monterey Peninsula, San Jose, Oakland, Stockton, Modesto, Fresno, Bakersfield, Los Angeles and Palm Springs, all in California, and to link Fresno and San Francisco to Medford and Portland in Oregon, and Boise (Idaho); there were

also services, mostly from Palm Springs but also from Portland and Boise, to Reno and Las Vegas in Nevada. Pacific Express regarded its One-Eleven operations as a natural 'lead-in' to beginning services with the British Aerospace BAe 146, of which it had six on order and eight on option. Sadly this order had to be cancelled when Pacific Express ceased operations in February 1984 because of losses due to the cut-throat competition in the California commuter markets and limited traffic. Three of its One-Elevens went to Cascade Airways and four to Air Wisconsin. Air Wisconsin's four, N101EX, N104EX, N105EX and N107EX, were acquired on lease from the British Jet Aircraft Co at the beginning of 1985, and supplement the airline's six BAe 146 Series 200s and 10 DHC-7 Dash 7s on commuter routes through Ohio, Michigan, Indiana, Illinois, Wisconsin, Minnesota and Nebraska. Another commuter airline, Florida Express, acquired three Series 203s from US Air, N1544, N1545 and N1548, plus N1543 a few months later, and began operations on 27 January 1984 when N1548 flew the first service from Indianopolis, Indiana, to Orlando, where the airline is based. These One-Elevens now link cities in Florida to Nashville (Tennessee), Louisville (Kentucky), Birmingham (Alabama), New Orleans (Louisiana), Cincinatti and Columbus (Ohio), and Indianapolis.

Another US commuter airline that recently introduced the One-Eleven was Air Illinois, which acquired the ex-Braniff Series 203 N1547 from US Air in July 1982. This operator flew a network linking places in southern Illinois to St Louis (Missouri) and Chicago, also serving Paducah (Kentucky) and Memphis (Tennessee), as well as Burlington (Iowa) and, just over the border in Missouri, Cape Girardeau and Quincy/Hannibal; Hannibal is famous for its association with Mark Twain. Air Illinois used a mixed fleet of BAe 748s and Jetstreams and DHC Twin Otters for the stopping services, and its One-Eleven flew

non-stop services from Chicago to Springfield and Evansville in southern Illinois and to St Louis. A second Series 203, N1542, was acquired from US Air just before both jets were grounded by the FAA in December 1983 for poor maintenance, and Air Illinois ceased operations. N1542 was later leased to Wright Airlines for six months from July 1984. As related earlier, Braniff had, early in 1972, sold off 11 of its One-Eleven 203s to Allegheny which was then about to merge with Mohawk, and Braniff also leased one for a short time in 1971 or 1972 to the Bahamas operator Flamingo Airways, which merged with Out Island Airways early in 1973 to form Bahamasair Holdings Ltd.

Braniff's first One-Eleven, N1541, was temporarily registered G-ASUF to BAC (Operating) Ltd to fly the Minister of Aviation, Mr Julian Amery, and a party of Ministry officials to a Concorde conference with the French at Sud Aviation's Melun Villaroche works on 6 July 1964. It later took part in the certification programme before delivery to Braniff, with whom it put in some seven years of hard short-haul work; after being leased out as N111QA it was returned to Braniff on 17 August 1972 as N541BN, and shortly after was sold to the Omni Investment Corp as N5LC, for use as an executive transport. The company sold it to the Amway Corp as N8LG early in 1976 and it later became N523AC.

After selling the rest of its One-Elevens to Allegheny, Braniff retained N1543 for its own use as an executive transport for a time, selling it to Air Chariot Ltd, which took delivery of it in March 1977. By 1978 it was owned by the Bermuda Learjet Corp and on 14 September that year had the Bermuda registration VR-BAC painted on, but these marks were never definitely allotted, and it reverted to N1543 the next day. By 1981 it was owned by Satellite Ltd, and late in 1982 it was sold to Cerro Industries Inc. It is now with Florida Express.

In Braniff, Mohawk and Allegheny service the One-Eleven had an excellent safety record, although Allegheny's N1550 was damaged in a landing accident at Rochester, New York on 9 July 1978, and was later written off. As mentioned previously, Allegheny (now US Air) has leased ex-Mohawk One-Eleven 204 N1117J to Quebecair, and N1120J to Pacific Express Inc. N1125J was sold in 1980 to the ONA Export Corp for executive use, and early in 1981 it was sold again to Saudi Wings, becoming HZ-MOI on 27 March that year. N1124J was temporarily registered G-AWDF on 13 February 1968 before delivery for trials in Spain.

The four ex-Laker Airways One-Eleven 320Ls were disposed of by B.Cal to a new Nigerian charter airline called Okada Air, being delivered from September 1983.

American and the One-Eleven 400

It was the American Airlines order for 15 One-Elevens plus 15 on option, announced on 17 July 1963 (a month before the prototype had flown) by the airline's president, Mr C. R. Smith, that really established the type as a potential world-beater in the eyes of the air transport industry. For Douglas had already, three months before, announced its decision to go ahead with the DC-9 jet, the One-Eleven's direct rival, and were committed to DC-9 production, with orders for 15 and three already in hand respectively from Delta Air Lines and Bonanza (which had originally wanted to order three One-Eleven 206s). This was the first time that a British airliner had been ordered 'off the drawing board' by a US airline when an alternative and directly comparable type of US design was available, and it was also the first time that one of the Big Four US domestic trunk carriers had ordered a British aircraft; it was also Britain's biggest single dollar export order ever. But what really made the order so significant and gratifying to BAC, and such a blow to Douglas and the DC-9 programme, was American's status and experience as a major sponsor airline; it had sponsored the world's most widely-used airliner, the famous Douglas DC-3, back in 1935, as well as the later DC-7, the Convair 240, the Lockheed Electra

Below:
American Airlines' fifth One-Eleven 401, N5019, was the 200th turbine-powered short haul airliner to be built by BAC for a North American customer, and the order from America was Britain's biggest single dollar export order ever.

turboprop and the Convair 990A medium-haul jet, and its requirements had been an important influence in the design of several other major transport types such as the Douglas DC-4 and DC-6 and Boeing 727.

So American carried immense prestige and commercial weight as a customer, and the airline had a long association going back many years with the Douglas company, having operated, as well as the DC-2, large fleets of the DC-3, DC-4, DC-6 and DC-6B and DC-7 over the years. The 14-passenger Douglas DC-2 of 1934 was, by the standards of its day, an important and very successful type but it did have some shortcomings, being somewhat underpowered and too small to carry a really economical payload. When a new 1,000hp version of the Wright Cyclone became available, American's vice-president engineering, William Littlewood, drew up, with the help of Otto Kirchner, a specification for a new and larger version of the DC-2 with these engines and a wider fuselage to take 12 sleeper berths as the DST (Douglas Sleeper Transport) for transcontinental routes, or 21 passenger seats in the so-called 'day plane' version, which became the DC-3. This specification was put before C. R. Smith, who liked it and decided to order 20, plus 20 more on option. But Donald Douglas was reluctant to go ahead with the new DC-3 and interrupt DC-2 deliveries, even though he had a backlog of 150 orders for the DC-2, an unprecedented total for an airliner at that time. But C. R. Smith was insistent, and finally persuaded

Douglas to accept his DC-3 order after a 2hr telephone call one evening in 1935; they exchanged telegrams the next morning confirming the order, but the contract was not legally finalised until the first 10 DC-3s had been delivered to American.

To recall this past history is to emphasise how close and personal was the relationship between American and Douglas, and what a wrench it must have been to C. R. Smith when, after 'extensive research and analysis going back to 1960', as he put it, his airline had to order a British jet for the very sort of routes that the DC-3, the Convair 240 and the Electra had been designed to operate. The technical choice between the DC-9 and One-Eleven was made after one of the most exhaustive technical analyses in American's history, and a key reason for the choice of the latter was that deliveries would have been possible about a year earlier than the DC-9; American was originally scheduled to receive its first One-Eleven in July 1965, although this was put back to December that year by the deep stall modifications. As Mr Smith said when announcing the order, 'we will receive all 15 airplanes before the first comparable airplane could be available to us from any other manufacturer'. Another important factor in its choice was the fact that, by the time American received its first One-Elevens, about 40 of the type would already have gone into airline service.

Also significant, and important in ensuring the One-Eleven's earlier delivery to the company, was American's decision to order the type with the standard Rolls-Royce Spey engine rather than with the Pratt & Whitney JT8D-5 turbofan which had been proposed for the One-Eleven; the latter engine also powered the 25 Boeing 727s American then had on order, and so there would have been obvious advantages in having it power the One-Eleven as well, but the delays that would have been incurred in fitting this engine to the One-Eleven and certificating this version would have largely nullified the earlier delivery

advantage. So American's One-Eleven 401s were delivered with the 11,000lb st Spey 510-14 turbofans, a derated version of the 11,400lb st Spey 511-14 which was standard for the Series 400, and to which standard the engines in American's Series 401s were later modified.

The maximum take-off weight of this version was at first restricted to 78,500lb and then 79,000lb to be below the US legal limit of 80,000lb for two-crew operation, but after this weight limit was lifted the Series 400 was certificated at 87,000lb and American's One-Elevens were in fact delivered with clearance to fly at 85,000lb. Now that the Series 400's take-off weight was the same as the Series 300's the latter version was no longer separately identified as such in new orders placed for the One-Eleven, since it was now identical to the Series 400, although those already built and sold as 300s (the Series 301s and 304s for British Eagle and Quebecair and the Series 320Ls for Laker) continued to be known as such. The Series 400 was now no longer intended mainly for North American operators, but was exported worldwide.

American's order was a serious blow to the embryo DC-9 programme, and Douglas put out a statement regretting AA's decision to 'buy an airplane built abroad and which we consider to be an inferior product to ours'. This brought a strong rejoinder from Mohawk president Mr Robert E. Peach, who wrote to Donald Douglas expressing 'absolute astonishment' at this statement.

'As a long-time user of Douglas products', wrote Mr Peach, 'and an early purchaser of the BAC One-Eleven, and also as one who has personally through many years unsuccessfully urged the Douglas Co to build a short-haul transport, I hope no responsible official of your company said it . . . if they did, I think it unnecessary to point out that American airframe manufacturers would be in sad shape indeed if many foreign carriers had not bought US . . . As to the quality of the product, I believe the record will speak for itself.'

Perhaps even more remarkable was what Mr Peach had to say to *Aviation Daily* in an interview at the time; his view was that US manufacturers:

'Have totally lost the ambition, if not the know-how, to build short-haul transport. I wish I could be paid for the man-hours that our company alone has spent in trying to interest each of the big four US manufacturers in building a short-haul transport during the past 15 years, yet to the best of my knowledge no sales representative of Douglas has ever so much as called upon our company.'

British industry had often been accused of indifferent salesmanship and failure to satisfy customers' needs in the past, and the aircraft industry was not wholly guiltless of this charge, but here was an American accusing his own countrymen in the very citadel of high-powered salesmanship and competitiveness of these very faults.

The One-Eleven 400 prototype G-ASYD made its first flight of 2hr 25min at Hurn on 13 July 1965, and was in fact the 301st short-haul turbine-powered airliner to be built there, following 21 One-Eleven 200s and 279 Viscounts; it underwent certification flight trials at BAC's Wisley flight test centre. It was followed into the air on 16 September by the second prototype, G-ASYE, a Series 410 originally intended to be N4111X for Page Airways International as an executive transport. The first Series 401 for American, N5015, first flew on 4 November 1965, and the One-Eleven 300/400

received its FAA Type Approval on 22 November and Air Registration Board certification on 10 December 1965. On 17 November G-ASYE left for the USA on the first part of a world demonstration tour, and was shown to seven airlines and 22 business organisations in the USA and Central America during the first 17 days of this tour, during which it made 68 flights. The forward part of the cabin was fitted out as an executive suite, designed by Charles Butler Associates of New York and installed by Marshalls Ltd of Cambridge to Page Airways International's requirements as the US distributor for executive One-Elevens; the rear of the cabin had airline-type seats. An executive suite such as this could include typically a conference area, a portable display area, a functional working lounge, sleeping accommodation or a bar, and in the rear of the cabin up to 20 first-class airline-type seats four-abreast.

After completing the first part of its tour, G-ASYE was loaned to American Airlines from 5 to 31 December for pilot training at New York, and this was followed by further demonstrations to 16 more business organisations and two airlines. G-ASYE returned to Wisley on 10 January 1966 after flying 261hr, of which 132 were on crew training, and covering over 50,000 miles. On 21 January G-ASYE left on the second part of its world tour, to Australia and New Zealand, in which it also gave demonstrations in Turkey, Iran, India, Ceylon (Sri Lanka), Burma, Thailand, the Philippines, Taiwan and Japan; it returned on 8 March after covering some 70,000 miles. It left the UK on 5 April to tour the South American countries, also giving demonstrations in the Bahamas and Trinidad, and returned on 1 May, having covered some 160,000 miles in the three parts of this world tour, and been demonstrated in 30 countries, making a total of 334 flights, of which only three were delayed for technical reasons. G-ASYE was sold as N3939V to the Victor Comptometer Corp of Chicago as an executive transport and left on delivery to the States on 8 September 1966.

American's first two One-Eleven 401s, N5015 and N5016, left on delivery through Prestwick on 23 and 22 December 1965 respectively; the airline now had 30 on order, having taken up in February 1964 10 of the 15 originally on option, and the remaining five later, the last of these being delivered on 16-17 December 1966. These had items of US design and manufacture replacing a number of the British-made pieces of equipment and parts usually fitted as standard, and an important US content in the instrumentation, gauges, navigational equipment and such things as hydraulic pumps and electric generators. For instance, Aerotherm Corp crew seats replaced the BAC ones, Bendix wheels and brakes were fitted in place of those by Dunlop, cabin windows were now made by Swedlow Inc of Los Angeles, and windscreens by the Pittsburgh Plate Glass Co of Pittsburgh, Pennsylvania.

American's One-Elevens were fitted out to seat 67 passengers, and were affectionately known as 'Baccalas' to AA's mechanics at the New York La Guardia base, although the airline's traffic and sales staff promoted them as Astrojet 400s. Their first services were flown between New York and Toronto on 6 March 1966, and by July/August that year they were making 1,200 departures a week from 22 airports drawing traffic from 25 states, the sector distances flown varying from 185 to 436 miles. AA's One-Elevens served eastern and mid-western cities, linking New York to Boston, Philadelphia and Washington DC, and to Chicago both via Detroit and through Washington, Cincinatti and Indianapolis. There were also services through Washington to Knoxville, Nashville and Memphis in Tennessee and Little Rock (Arkansas), and through Nashville to Tulsa, Oklahoma City and Dallas, linking up here with the Braniff One-Eleven network. AA's Astrojet 400s also linked Oklahoma City, Tulsa and St Louis (Missouri) to Chicago. American's One-Eleven passenger load factors were 69% in May 1966, 75% in June and no less than 81% during the week ending 2 July – indicative of the aircraft's great passenger appeal over propeller-driven types – and block time utilisation was 9hr 33min daily. Like Braniff and Mohawk, American found its

One-Elevens very reliable, and during March (the first month in service) and June they recorded fewer engineering delays than any other turbine-powered types in AA's fleet.

Early in 1967 American used its One-Elevens to launch a concerted attack on the New York-Boston route, a market worth $30million yearly with a potential of about two million passengers; in January that year American had claimed only a paltry 3% of this big market, carrying 5,000 passengers between the two cities. On 12 February AA introduced 'Jet Express' services between New York La Guardia and Boston's Logan Airport, with a One-Eleven leaving both cities every hour on the half-hour 16 times a day from early morning to late evening; 15,000 seats weekly were provided over this 185-mile route, of which 10,000 were at the low $16 coach fare, and the rest first class. Altogether 14,473 passengers were carried in the first 11 days of Jet Express services at an average 68% load factor, and by October 1967 AA's share of the New York-Boston market had risen sharply to 24%, with over 35,000 passengers a month being carried over this route; by this time AA's Astrojet 400s had carried more than 3½ million passengers since going into service. The success of 'Jet Express' services between New York and Boston led to similar high frequency services under the same name between New York and Washington. American had 19% of this market in June 1967 when it carried about 29,000 passengers, but when Jet Express services were introduced AA's share of the market rose to 27%, and in August 37,000 passengers were carried between New York La Guardia and Washington.

On both these Jet Express routes AA's Astrojet 400s proved they could increase the share of the market against strong competition from larger jets. This was also true of the Boston-Washington non-stop route; during June 1967 American scheduled 13 Astrojet 400 flights and one Boeing 727 flight daily between the two cities against powerful competition from Northeast Airlines and Eastern, which between them scheduled 19 Boeing 727 flights and six Electra flights daily. But despite this, AA's Astrojet 400 load factor was no less than

86% in June, 81% in May, 82% in July and 84% in August – sure evidence of the type's ability to compete.

The One-Eleven was able to offset its disadvantage of being smaller by the high frequencies that its self-contained nature and independence of ground services made possible, and by excellent reliability. AA's One-Eleven co-ordinator, Bruce Jobson, described it neatly as 'an instant aeroplane', adding 'It is operationally self supporting . . . well built and well thought out. It's a quality product'. It was also proving, in US airline service, to be cheaper to operate than the competition, returning lower aircraft-mile and seat-mile costs than the rival DC-9, and lower seat-mile costs than the piston-engined Convair 440s and 240s it replaced on a number of routes. It also attracted comfortably higher load factors than either the DC-9 or the Boeing 737 during the first half of 1969, as it had done since the beginning of 1967, even though by this time both the rival US short-haul jets were well established in airline service, and might have been expected to attract a greater brand loyalty from the American travelling public.

Executive Resales

Most of American's One-Eleven 401s were sold off as executive transports, although a few went to other airlines. N5041 and N5044 were sold to Dan-Air Services Ltd as G-AXCP and G-AXCK respectively, being delivered to London Gatwick in March 1969. N5026 went to Orientair Ltd as G-AZMI

for a proposed inclusive tour operation from West Berlin for the German tour operator GUT, but this was not started and G-AZMI went into storage shortly after it was delivered to Hurn on 29 January 1972, later becoming G-BBME with British Airways Regional Division. N5035 was delivered to Tarom of Rumania on 20 June 1972 as YR-BCG to supplement that airline's Series 424s, and four Series 401s were sold to Bahamasair Holdings Ltd in 1973. The first of these was N5032 which became VP-BDI; this had been temporarily registered to BAC as G-ATVU in June 1966 before delivery for a demonstration in Sweden. It was later leased by American to the Indonesian airline Merpati Nusantara Airlines for three months of trial operations over domestic routes from 11 August 1971, and in 1973 it did a further spell on lease to LANICA of Nicaragua as AN-BHN, before going to Bahamasair. The latter's other three Series 401s were N5022, N5023 and N5043, which became VP-BDN, VP-BDP and VP-BDJ respectively.

The first Series 401 to be sold as an executive transport had been N5031 in April 1969, which went to the Farmland Corp of Vicksburg, Mississippi, as N111FL; after a few months in the corporation's service it was sold to Magnolia Homes and then to F. L. Cappaert (later the Cappaert Investment Corp), and by 1976 it had become N5LC of the Stewart Lumber Co. In March 1984 it was sold to Lone Star Industries. But it was not until 1973 that American disposed of most of the remainder of its One-Eleven 401 fleet when National Aircraft Leasing Ltd of Chicago – NAL, a member of the Tiger Leasing Group – bought two

Below:
American's first One-Eleven 401, N5015, seen at Hurn before delivery on 23 December 1965. The AA aircraft had items of US design and manufacture replacing a number of British-made parts, such as Bendix wheels and brakes in place of Dunlop ones.

Right:
VP-BDI was one of four AA One-Eleven 401s sold to Bahamasair Holdings Ltd in 1973 for use on inter-island services and the routes to Florida; it was formerly N5032.
D. Spurgeon via J. M. G. Gradidge

Series 401s with an option (soon taken up) on 16 more, for lease or resale as executive transports. The BAC jet had already proved itself in this role; its self-contained features made it possible to operate from small airfields or company airstrips without the facilities of a major airport, it could carry about 25 senior executives in a luxury interior and, if so desired, the rear part of the cabin could be fitted with about 20 airline-type seats four-abreast, while extra fuel tankage could be installed to give non-stop transcontinental or intercontinental range. National Aircraft Leasing took delivery of the Series 401s during 1973-74, they were leased or resold by NAL and Tiger Air to corporate customers in the States. Most have passed through the hands of two or three different owners since.

NAL showed the executive Series 401 N111NA (ex-N5025) in the static park at the 1974 SBAC Show at Farnborough, and at the 1975 Paris Salon at le Bourget; also present on the latter occasion was the Carver Corp's executive One-Eleven 422 N18814, formerly PP-SRT of VASP. N111NA later went to Allis Chalmers as N825AC, and in 1982 was sold to McMoran Properties Inc as N117MR. N5024 was used by Governor George Wallace of Alabama to tour the country as a Presidential candidate in the 1976 campaign, and for this became N76GW *Trust The People*. It was later sold to the National Commercial Bank of Saudi Arabia as HZ-NB2, being delivered on 18 February 1978. This was one of several One-Eleven 401s to go to Saudi Arabia, which is now the biggest executive user of the type outside the United States. N5017 went to Norton Simon Inc as N277NS; the company sold it after nine years in service to the CAW Corp in January 1983, and in May it received the Cayman Islands registration VR-CBI for a new owner, Bryan Aviation. Early in 1984 N5034 became VR-BHS of Air Hanson/Air St George Ltd, while in June that year N5033 was delivered as A6-SHJ to one of the United Arab Emirates.

Another Series 401 to go to Saudi Arabia was the former N5020 which, after going to Tiger Leasing as N111NA (one of three to use this registration), later became N102GP; it was sold as HZ-GRP to the Saudi Research & Development Corp, being delivered to it on 15 January 1976 through Gander and Gatwick. It later became HZ-GP2 and, after sale to the Saudi National Commercial Bank, was re-registered HZ-NB3 in October 1979, becoming HZ-MAA later. Another that went to Saudi Arabia was N5029, which was sold to the Louis Luyt Group of South Africa and registered in Swaziland as 3D-LLG; it became VR-CAM in November 1977 and the following April was delivered to Sheikh Baroon of Jeddah as HZ-AMB *Nawaf*. N5038 was sold to Jet Travel Inc of Oklahoma City as N10HM on 17 January 1973 and immediately leased to Cimaron Industries, going to Rogers Bros in June 1974; some time later it became N90TF of the Omni Corporation and in 1982 went to a Saudi Arabian customer as HZ-MFA, later becoming HZ-BLI. Two more Saudi exports were N5039 and N5042, both of which were leased by NAL for a time in 1978 to Austral of Argentina, as related in the next chapter. In July 1980 N5039 was acquired by the Al Jabalain Trading & Investment Co as HZ-RHI, and was delivered to Hurn on 27 July with both US and Saudi registrations carried; three years later it became HZ-HRI on its sale to the Civil Construction Establishment. N5042 went to the First National Bank as N112NA in May 1974, later reverting to NAL; late in 1980 it became HZ-NIR of Rashid Engineering, being re-registered HZ-MAJ in June 1983.

The Series 400 Sells Widely

Next customer for the Series 400 after American was Philippine Air Lines Inc, for whom an order for two 74-passenger One-Eleven 402s was announced on 3 November 1964, plus a third on option; this was taken up in December 1966, and a fourth was ordered on 9 June 1967, plus one more on option. The first, PI-C1121, was delivered to Manila on 19 April 1966 followed by the second, PI-C1131, on 24 September. One-Eleven services began on 1 May that year, linking Manila to the cities of Bacolod, Mactan and Davao, and flying from the Philippine capital to Hong Kong and Taipei (Taiwan); a fourth domestic destination, the city of Iloilo, was added to the One-Eleven network on 6 May 1967. The first aircraft, PI-C1121, flew from 8hr 18min to 8hr 54min daily until the second arrived, with a very low technical delay rate of 0.3% of departures and zero in two successive months. During their first year of revenue service the PALjets, as the airline called them, carried 87,000 passengers on domestic routes, and in 1968 they opened a third international route from Manila to Saigon, followed by another in 1969 from Manila via Cebu to the Indonesian island of Bali (Denpasar); both the Saigon and Bali routes were flown once-weekly.

PI-C1131 crashed a few miles from Manila International Airport on 12 September 1969 with the loss of all but two of the 47 people on board, while the third, PI-C1141, after becoming G-16-1 and G-AVEJ with BAC, was leased to the German charter airline Bavaria Fluggesellschaft, to which it was delivered on 23 February 1967, returning from

lease that October and being delivered to Manila the following month. Although the registration D-AFWB was allotted to it, this was not taken up, as it was contrary to German law for a leased aircraft to wear German marks, and it was used by Bavaria as G-AVEJ pending delivery of its first One-Eleven 414. After PAL's three Series 402s had been replaced by its first three One-Eleven 527s in 1971, PI-C1121 was returned to BAC for resale in January 1972, and later went to Quebecair as CF-QBR, as previously related. The fourth One-Eleven 402, PI-C1151, was not in fact delivered to PAL and instead was acquired by the Spanish charter operator TAE – Trabajos Aereos y Enlaces – to which it was delivered as EC-BQF on 1 March 1969. TAE operated it for over a year but it was returned to BAC and registered to the company as G-AYHM in July 1970; it was then leased to Bavaria in August, returning on 4 January 1971, and later went into storage at Hurn, being sold to TAROM of Rumania in August 1972 as YR-BCH. PAL's first One-Eleven, PI-C1121, was sold to the Ministry of Defence (Aviation) in 1974 as XX919 for use as a 'flying laboratory' by the RAE's Avionics Flight & Radio Department at Farnborough. Here it was used for a wide range of advanced programmes, including research into different aspects of satellite communications.

The first of three Central American national airlines to order One-Eleven 400s was TACA International Airlines SA of El Salvador, which announced an order for two Series 407s plus two more on option in November 1965. TACA had

PI-C1131

previously operated a total of six Viscount 700s, putting its first – actually a Viscount 784 leased from Philippine Air Lines – into service on 25 November 1957. The airline's first One-Eleven 407, YS-17C *El Centroamericano*, was delivered on 14 December 1966 and was followed by YS-18C *El Salvador* on 21 February 1967. They were joined by a third (Series 409 TI-1056C acquired from LACSA of Costa Rica in September 1969) which became YS-01C *El Izalco*. TACA's One-Elevens operated services, which started in December 1966, from San Salvador to Guatemala City, Belize (capital of British Honduras, now the state of Belize), Managua (Nicaragua), San Jose (Costa Rica) and Panama City, and also to Mexico City and New Orleans, Louisiana. One-Eleven YS-01C was sold back to British Aerospace in 1979 as G-BGTU, which sold it to Turbo Union Ltd of Filton, which manages the RB.199 engine programme for the Panavia Tornado.

LACSA of Costa Rica (Lineas Aereas Costarricenses SA) announced an order for one One-Eleven 409 plus one on option on 19 January 1966, and inaugurated services with this, TI-1056C, between San Jose (the Costa Rican capital) and Miami on 14 May 1967; the new 150min jet schedule between these two cities cut 2hr off the previous flight time with piston-engined DC-6Bs. The first One-Eleven was named *El Tico* – a central American colloquialism for the Costa Rican – and was soon linking the capital to San Salvador, Mexico City, Panama City and to Grand Cayman in the Cayman Islands, some 200 miles south of Cuba and west of Jamaica; these islands are best known today as a tax haven. *El Tico* was replaced after its sale as YS-01C by the second One-Eleven 409, TI-1055C, in November 1969; this had first flown on 14 February as G-16-6 and soon became G-AXBB with BAC for a short lease to Quebecair, followed by another period on lease to TAROM of Rumania as YR-BCP. It returned from this lease in August to be re-registered G-AXBB for another short lease to Germanair of Munich prior to delivery to LACSA. After LACSA's One-Eleven 531s were in service, TI-1055C was returned to BAC in January 1974, becoming G-AXBB again and later being sold to Gulf Aviation.

LANICA of Nicaragua (Lineas Aereas de Nicaragua SA) was the last of the three Central American carriers to announce an order for the One-Eleven, which it did on 6 April 1966 for one Series 412 plus one on option, but was the first to put the type into service. This it did by leasing Series 208 EI-ANF *St Malachy* from Aer Lingus as AN-BBS for six months pending delivery of the Series 412. The Series 208 left Dublin for LANICA on 29 October 1966, stopping at Goose Bay and Miami, and on 1 November inaugurated jet services from Managua, the Nicaraguan capital, to Miami via San Salvador; it was returned to Aer Lingus after LANICA's Series 412 AN-BBI was delivered on 20 April 1967, and from 1 May this went into service on routes from Managua to San Salvador and Mexico City, as well as to Miami.

On 19 October that year a lease agreement was signed providing for the joint operation of the One-Eleven 412 by LANICA and TAN Airlines of Honduras (Transportes Aereos Nacionales SA), and a unique feature of this was that the agreement was signed by the Presidents of the two countries concerned, General Anastasio Somoza of Nicaragua and Colonel Oswaldo Lopez of Honduras; other Central American airlines were also invited to join LANICA in similar joint operation of the One-Eleven. The Somoza family

Below left:
Philippine Air Lines used three One-Eleven 402s – of which the second, PI-C1131 is seen here, on its major domestic routes and on routes from Manila to Hong Kong, Taipei (Taiwan), Saigon and Bali.

Below:
The third PAL One-Eleven 402, PI-C1141, became G-16-1 and G-AVEJ with BAC for lease to Bavaria Fluggesellschaft from 23 February to October 1967, pending delivery of Bavaria's first One-Eleven 414.

had then been in power for some 30 years and ran not only the country and its Army, but its airline, shipping lines and many other commercial interest. TAN Airlines used the One-Eleven 412 to inaugurate non-stop services between San Pedro Sula, Honduras, and Miami on 1 November 1967, this being the first non-stop jet service between Honduras and the USA; the One-Eleven cut flight times between the two cities from 4hr to 2hr, and TAN Airlines planned to use it to serve San Salvador, Belize City (Belize) and Mexico City. TAN Airlines' joint operation with LANICA, and Aviateca of Guatemala's first order for the One-Eleven 516 placed late in 1970, meant that the British jet was to equip the national carriers of all five countries forming the Central American Common Market. LANICA also leased One-Eleven 401 N5032 as AN-BHN for several months in 1973, and had previously leased Series 518 G-AXML from Court Line as AN-BHJ from December 1971 to 28 March 1972. One-Eleven AN-BBI was sold in 1975 when it was replaced by a Boeing 727 and became N221CN and then N767RV as an executive transport with the Revlon Corp cosmetics business. It was sold to IASCO Inc early in 1979, which soon sold it as N90AM to AMM Inc; by October that year it had changed hands again to a Saudi Arabian customer as HZ-JAM.

First British independent to order the Series 400 had been British Eagle International Airlines, which in 1965 ordered three One-Eleven 406s for operations starting in the summer of 1966, with three more on option. But when the opportunity arose to acquire the three Kuwait Airways Series 301s and the two Central African Airways Series 207s for delivery at the same time this order was cancelled. Channel Airways was the first British independent to operate the Series 400, having announced an order for four One-Eleven 408s on 5 September 1966, and taken an option on two more; this option was taken up the following May but

later lapsed. Channel's One-Elevens were for use on routes from Southend to Ostend, Rotterdam, Paris and the Channel Islands, and on IT charter flights to a number of European destinations; an 89-passenger cabin interior was featured.

The first Series 408, G-AVGP, was delivered on 14 June 1967 and the second, G-AWEJ, on 10 May 1968. The first was allotted the Dominican registration HI-148 for a proposed lease in 1968 to the national airline Cia Dominicana de Aviacion, C. por A., and it was actually painted in its livery in June that year, but the lease fell through and G-AVGP was not delivered, Dominicana acquiring a DC-9 Series 32 instead. Early in 1969 G-AVGP was leased to Autair International for a time at weekends to supplement its Series 416s at these peak traffic periods. Channel's third One-Eleven, G-AWGG, was registered to BAC on 19 June 1968 and leased to Bavaria Fluggesellschaft as a Series 413, being delivered on 25 June and returning from lease in December. It was then leased to Austral/ALA of Argentina, being painted in ALA livery, and in February 1969 it was sold to Bavaria as D-ALLI. Channel's fourth Series 408, G-AWKJ, was delivered straight away on lease to British United on 3 April 1969 to replace British United's Series 201 G-ASJJ that had crashed on take-off at Milan in January.

These various leases and resales were partly explained by Channel beginning to feel the financial strains of expansion; it took delivery of two Trident 1E-140s in 1968 and the first of five ex-BEA Comet 4Bs at the end of 1969 to supplement its One-Elevens, nine Viscount 812s and three HS.748s, and the main operating base had been transferred from Southend to Stansted with the introduction of jets. But this multiplicity of types helped bring about the financial difficulties that led Channel to cease operations and go into receivership in February 1972. When this happened, G-AWKJ, now returned from BUA, was

Far left:
The fourth One-Eleven 402 for PAL, PI-C1151, was not after all delivered to the Philippines, but became EC-BQF *Nervion* with the Spanish charter operator Trabajos Aereos y Enlaces on 1 March 1969. TAE operated it for over a year before returning it to BAC.

Left:
YS-17C *El Centroamericano* seen here was the first of two One-Eleven 407s for TACA International Airlines SA of El Salvador, which also acquired a Series 409 from LACSA. The Salvadorean flag on the fin is blue, white and blue, and under the fuselage flash are the words 'Transportes Aereos Centro Americanos'.

put into storage at Hurn, and was later acquired by Air Hanson Helicopters Ltd, being re-registered G-BIII in the company's name in January 1974. It was delivered through Prestwick to Newark, New Jersey on 18 February that year for refitting as an executive transport, and in July became RP-C1 of the Central Bank of the Philippines. It was also used as a VIP transport by the Philippine Air Force's 702nd Squadron of the 700th Special Mission Wing. It was sold back to the UK and flown to London Gatwick in February 1984. Series 408 G-AWEJ was sold to British Airways Regional Division in September 1973 as G-BBMG for use on the Scottish routes; it was named *County of Gloucestershire* in 1983. G-AVGP, after a spell on lease to Autair International from BAC as *Halcyon Cloud*, was sold to Cambrian Airways Ltd in December 1969.

Bavaria Fluggesellschaft of Munich was the first of several European charter and IT operators to order the One-Eleven 400, an order for two Series 414s plus one on option being announced on 30 November 1966; this option was later taken up and one more ordered on 5 June 1969. As related earlier, operations started with the Philippine Air Lines Series 402 PI-C1141 leased through BAC as G-AVEJ, which was delivered on 23 February 1967 and used until October that year pending delivery of the first Series 414 D-ANDY, which had first flown as G-16-3, on 29 December. G-AVEJ was sub-leased to Lufthansa for six weeks from 1 April 1967, flying eight services daily for it, linking Munich and Frankfurt to Geneva, Vienna and Hamburg. Channel's G-AWGG was also leased from June to December 1968 and sold to Bavaria in February 1969 as D-ALLI. This was followed by the

Left:
LACSA of Costa Rica's first One-Eleven 409, TI-1056C, was named *El Tico*, which is Central American slang for the Costa Rican. It is seen here at San Jose's El Coco International Airport in a typical Latin American environment of DC-3 and C-46 operations.

Right:
The two LACSA One-Elevens carried the badge of the Carretas, or traditional Costa Rican farm cart wheel, on the fin, and the red, white and blue national flag on the rear fuselage. TI-1056C was later sold to TACA International as YS-01C *El Izalco.*

Bottom:
LANICA (Lineas Aereas de Nicaragua SA) put One-Eleven 412 AN-BBI into service in May 1967 on international routes to replace One-Eleven 208 AN-BBS which it had leased from Aer Lingus. Later AN-BBI was operated jointly with TAN Airlines of Honduras.

Far right:
G-AVGP was the first of four One-Eleven 408s for Channel Airways' scheduled services and inclusive tour flights from Southend and Stansted. However, in the end only two of these were actually operated by Channel.

third, fourth and fifth Series 414s, D-AILY, D-AISY and D-ANNO, delivered on 26 February, 22 April and 22 December 1970. Series 402 G-AYHM was also leased from August to the end of 1970.

From May to October 1968 the first two, fitted out to seat 84 passengers, were operating IT charter flights from Munich, Stuttgart, Nuremburg, Frankfurt and Dusseldorf to 15 destinations in the Mediterranean and the UK. These were Malaga, Barcelona and Palma in Spain, Bastia in Corsica, Tunis in North Africa, Rimini and Naples in Italy, Dubrovnik in Yugoslavia, Athens, Constanta on the Rumanian Black Sea coast and, in the UK, London Gatwick, Luton, Manchester, Newcastle and Glasgow. The two One-Elevens were flying 64 sectors a week in the summer of 1968, totalling 52,000 miles and 136hr, the average flight time being 1hr 40min and flight length 650 miles. An average utilisation of 10hr daily was achieved, the peak utilisation at weekends rising to 15hr per day. Unlike most British One-Eleven IT charter operators, Bavaria did not generally sell the whole

capacity of its aircraft on any flight to one tour operator, but to several on the same flight; in the 1968 season a total of 18 German travel firms were offering holiday flights in Bavaria's One-Elevens, whereas British independents tended to have two or three major tour operators as their main IT customers. Bavaria's first two One-Elevens also continued to operate scheduled domestic flights for Lufthansa in 1968 between Munich and Hanover. Palma in Majorca was Bavaria's most popular One-Eleven destination in 1968, with seven flights a week; the type was very popular with German passengers, so much so that spontaneous outbreaks of applause from the cabin after a One-Eleven landing were not unusual.

After Bavaria's One-Eleven 515s were delivered, the Series 414s were gradually sold off, D-ANDY going to Dan-Air Services Ltd as G-AZED, being delivered to them on 21 December 1971. The ex-Channel D-ALLI was leased to Gulf Aviation of Bahrain from late 1975 to April 1977, retaining its German registration. It was later sold to Air Pacific

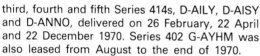

Ltd of Suva, Fiji to supplement that company's two One-Eleven 479s, and became DQ-FCR, being delivered via Bahrain on 29 June 1978. It flew regional services for Air Pacific but was grounded by corrosion late in 1980, and as a result withdrawn from use. Series 414s D-AILY, D-AISY and D-ANNO were all sold as executive transports, the first being delivered through Prestwick to the USA on 6 December 1975 and becoming N123H of Hilton Hotels. D-AISY which, in spite of its registration, was actually named *Franz von Lenbach*, was sold late in 1977 to Saudi Arabia, becoming HZ-AMH of the A. M. Hassawi Group, which later sold it to Abdul Aziz Al Ibrahim as HZ-ABI. D-ANNO was sold to the Ford Motor Co as G-BFMC, and in 1978 joined the two ex-Brazilian Air Force One-Eleven 423s in Ford's Stansted-based private airline, flying company personnel to plants on the Continent.

The Brazilian Government order for two One-Eleven 423s for the Forca Aerea Brasileira's Special Transport Group was announced on 19 November 1967, and they were for use by the President, government ministers and other VIPs. The first flew with the BAC Class B registration G-16-2, and was delivered on 15 October 1968 with the Brazilian military serial VC92-2111, while the second one first flew as G-16-4 and was delivered from Weybridge on 13 May 1969 as VC92-2110. They both had a 700lmp gal long-range fuel tank and were based at Brasilia, the capital, with other types in the Special Transport Group (Grupo de Transporte Especial), which included a Viscount 742 and some Hawker-Siddeley HS.125 executive jets; the One-Elevens served until 1976, when they were sold to the Ford Motor Co Ltd after being replaced by two Boeing 737-200s. VC92-2111 became G-BEJM and was delivered to Stansted on

17 December 1976 while VC92-2110, delivered to Stansted on the following day, became G-BEJW. They were later joined in the Ford fleet by the ex-Bavaria G-BFMC. Apart from the two Brazilian Air Force ones, only one other Series 400 was built specifically for executive or VIP use; this was One-Eleven 419 N270E for Engelhard Industries, a precious metals company of New York, and had been acquired through the US executive distributors Page Airways International and delivered on 21 September 1967; it had a 1,000 lmp gal auxiliary fuel system and was later sold to the Rockwell Manufacturing Co as N44R. The second prototype Series 400 G-ASYE had been sold to the Victor Comptometer Corp of Chicago, makers of business machines, as N3939V for executive use after completing its worldwide sales and demonstration tours of November 1965-May 1966. The Victor company finally sold it, and by 1978 it had become N77CS of Chessie Services Inc and then N77QS. It was sold to Saudi Arabia and on 9 April 1979 it was registered HZ-AMK to AMK Ltd for the use of Sheikh Abdul Maksoud Khotah. It was sold to the USA early in 1984.

First South American customer for the One-Eleven was Aerocondor – Aerovias Condor de Colombia Ltda – of Barranquilla, which operated domestic routes and services to Miami, Aruba and Curacao. An order for one Series 400 for Aerocondor was announced on 29 April 1966; during demonstrator G-ASYE's round-the-world tour Aerocondor's pilots, with no previous jet experience, had flown it with complete satisfaction from Bogota Airport, which was 8,355ft above sea level. But despite this the Aerocondor order lapsed, and the One-Eleven was never delivered. The first Brazilian One-Eleven customer was Viacao Aerea

Top:
G-AVGP is seen here in the livery of Cia Dominicana de Aviacion C por A for a proposed lease in mid-1968 that fell through when the Dominican airline acquired a DC-9 Series 32. The One-Eleven was allotted the Dominican registration HI-148, but this was not taken up.

Above centre:
G-AVGP in the livery of Cambrian Airways Ltd, to whom it was sold in December 1969 after a spell with Autair International as *Halcyon Cloud.* Cambrian was later integrated into British Airways Regional Division.
Austin J. Brown

Above:
VC-92 2111 was one of the two One-Eleven 423s of the Brazilian Air Force's Special Transport Group based at Brasilia, and used as VIP transports for the President and government ministers. These two jets had a 700Imp gal long range fuel tank and Doppler navigation systems.

São Paulo SA – VASP – which announced an order for two Series 422s, plus three more on option, on 22 June 1967. VASP had been founded in 1933 to provide air transport from Sao Paulo, capital of the state of that name, to other parts of Brazil; most of the airline's stock was held by the state's government, the state bank and the municipality of Sao Paulo. VASP had introduced turboprops when the first of five Viscount 827s was delivered in October 1958, and nine Viscount 701s were later acquired from BEA.

The two 74-passenger One-Eleven 422s, PP-SRT and PP-SRU, were both delivered via Prestwick on the same day, 19 December 1967, and entered service in January. During their first year's operation, as part of a mixed fleet of 38 aircraft which included the Viscounts and older piston-engined types, the One-Elevens accounted for no less than 24% of VASP's passenger-miles flown. By 1969 the two jets were flying 92 sectors a week, totalling 51,000 miles and 119hr flown, an average utilisation of 8.5hr daily being achieved by each One-Eleven. Sector lengths varied from the 1,526 miles of the Rio de Janeiro to Belem route, and the 804 miles from Belem near the mouth of the Amazon to Manaus nearly half way along this great river, to the 237 miles of the Rio-Sao Paulo route.

One of the BAC jets flew from Sao Paulo to Rio, on to Belem and down to Manaus and back during a day's work, while the other flew from Porto Alegre in the far south of the country, to Sao Paulo and Rio, and from there along the coastal route around the 'shoulder' of Brazil to Salvador, Recife and Fortaleza. Leaving Fortaleza at 07.30hrs, the One-Eleven would arrive at Porto Alegre at 15.05hrs and, departing from there at 15.45hrs on the same route, would be back at Fortaleza at 22.55hrs. By January 1969 the two jets had completed a year of operations without a single in-flight engine shutdown or unscheduled engine removal, while less than 2% of scheduled departures had been delayed for technical reasons. On 25 July that year VASP took delivery of its first

four Boeing 737-200s, and as more of these were put into service (eventually more than 20 were acquired, replacing the older propeller-driven types) the One-Elevens were relegated to less important routes and were finally sold in 1974, returning to BAC in May and June that year. Both were refurbished as executive transports and sold to the Carver Corporation later that year, PP-SRT becoming N18814 and PP-SRU becoming N18813. In 1979 the latter was sold to the Tracinda Investment Corp as N341TC, and two years later was disposed of to Gas Source Inc as N111GS. It was sold as A6-RKT to the Government of Ras Al Khaimah, one of the United Arab Emirates, being delivered on 19 October 1984. The former PP-SRT is now N114M of Montex Drilling.

It was Austral/ALA of Argentina that was to be the largest South American customer for the One-Eleven, and the only one to operate Series 400s and Series 500s. Austral (Compania Argentina de Transportes Aereos SA Cel) ordered four Series 420s in May 1967 for joint operation on domestic routes with its partner ALA – Aerotransportes Litoral Argentino SA. ALA, in which Austral had acquired a 30% holding in 1966, had been formed in 1957 and concentrated on operating short-haul routes radiating from Rosario, 180 miles northwest of Buenos Aires in Santa Fe province. After Austral had acquired a holding in it, ALA's operations were increasingly integrated with those of the larger carrier, and a merger of the two airlines was a logical step. This took place in June 1971 to form Austral Lineas Aereas SA; until then the airlines were known jointly as Austral/ALA. The original Austral had also been formed in 1957 and its major

Above:
PP-SRT was the first of two One-Eleven 422s for VASP of Sao Paulo, which started services with them in January 1968. They flew the coastal route around the 'shoulder' of Brazil, and from Belem near the mouth of the Amazon down to Manaus.

route was the trunk route down the Patagonian coast to Rio Grande in Tierra del Fuego; in the far south Punta Arenas on the Chilean side of the Magellan Straits was also served, and there were also routes to Montevideo (Uruguay) and Asuncion (Paraguay). Austral had started operating the Patagonian route with Curtiss C-46s which were replaced by second-hand Douglas DC-6s and DC-6Bs (mostly ex-American Airlines), of which about a dozen were acquired from 1964.

It was to replace these that the 74-passenger One-Eleven 420s were ordered, the first two being delivered on 12 October and 8 November 1967 with, as is the Argentine practice, 'provisional' registrations LV-PID and LV-PIF respectively, the former to become LV-IZR on arrival and the latter LV-IZS. This was temporarily registered G-AVTF to BAC for a demonstration to Tarom of Rumania in May 1967. The next two followed a year later, LV-PKB leaving Gatwick on delivery on 24 September 1968 to become LV-JGX later, and LV-PKA (later LV-JGY) leaving on 17 December. One-Eleven services (the first by this jet in South America) began in November 1967, and by 1969 the jets were serving 18 Argentine towns and cities, and also Asuncion in Paraguay and Puerto Montt and Antofagasta in Chile. With the delivery of the third aircraft, ALA began to operate One-Eleven services over some of its routes in September 1968.

After a year's operations, public demand for seats on the One-Elevens was such that it became necessary to lease a fifth aircraft, the Channel Airways Series 408 G-AWGG, for a few weeks in January 1969 (which is the peak summer period in the southern hemisphere) prior to its sale to Bavaria the following month. In typical Argentine summer operations each of the five One-Elevens averaged eight flights daily, flying over 3,000 miles on sectors ranging from 138 to over 880 miles in length. Apart from the Patagonian trunk route from Buenos Aires via Bahia Blanca, Trelew and the oil port of Comodoro Rivadavia to Rio Gallegos in the far south, Austral/ALA served Neuquen and the ski resort of San Carlos de Bariloche in central Argentina, as well as routes radiating westward from Buenos Aires to Mendoza, San Juan and Cordoba and northwards to as far north as Tucuman and Salta. The Series 420s continued to serve Austral/ALA for some years after the airline's first One-Eleven 521s were delivered, but LV-JGY crashed near San Carlos de Bariloche on 21 November 1977 with the loss of 45 people on board; not long after, on 27 January 1978, LV-JGX was badly damaged at Buenos Aires Aeroparque airport when a fire occurred during replenishment of the oxygen system, and in 1979 it was sold to Omni Aviation. To make up the capacity lost with these two aircraft, a pair of ex-American Airlines One-Eleven 401s, N5039 and N5042, were leased for a time in 1978 from National Aircraft Leasing of Chicago. As related earlier, LV-IZR and LV-IZS, after being returned to BAC in February 1981 and October 1980 respectively, were later leased to Quebecair as C-GQBP and C-GQBV.

The next British independent after Channel Airways to choose the One-Eleven 400 was Autair International Airways Ltd, which announced an order for two Series 416s on 25 February 1967, a third later and two more in mid-1968. The first of these, G-AVOE *Halcyon Days*, was delivered on 8 February 1968, and was followed by G-AVOF *Halcyon Breeze* on 19 March, G-AWBL *Halcyon Dawn* on 1 May 1968 and G-AWXJ *Halcyon Sun* on 20 March 1969. The fifth aircraft, instead of a new

Above:
The first of four One-Eleven 420s for Austral of Argentina is seen before delivery in its 'provisional' registration LV-PID before becoming LV-IZR. Austral used these four on its Patagonian trunk route down to Tierra del Fuego in the far south, as well as on other routes to the western and northern parts of Argentina.

Series 416, was G-AVGP leased from Channel early in 1969, initially just for the peak weekend periods, and later bought from Channel through BAC and named *Halcyon Cloud*.

The One-Elevens were used for inclusive tour flights from Luton to European holiday destinations for several important tour operators such as Clarksons Holidays, Pontinental, Wallace Arnold and Jetway, Clarksons being the most important customer. During August 1969 one of the One-Elevens set up what was claimed to be a world record in utilisation for the type by flying 402hr 36min during the month, or an average daily figure of 13hr; several One-Eleven IT operators had achieved 15hr a day at peak weekend periods, but this fell away to 10hr or less during weekdays. The Series 416s had accommodation for 86 passengers, and an innovation introduced by Autair was the provision of a pre-packed meal already in the seat back on take-off so that passengers could eat when they felt like it rather than have to wait for the cabin staff to bring their meal to them. With the delivery of the first One-Eleven 518s from December 1969, three of the Series 416s and the ex-Channel G-AVGP were sold to Cambrian Airways Ltd from December and Autair changed its name to Court Line (Aviation) Ltd with effect from 1 January 1970, taking its title from the shipping line of which it had been a wholly-owned subsidiary since April 1965.

Cambrian Airways from 1946 began to fly scheduled services from Cardiff, developing routes domestically and to the Channel Islands, Paris and Ireland; BEA's short-haul routes from the Isle of Man were taken over in 1962, and in 1968 Cambrian became the sole operator of the London-Liverpool route. In March that year Cambrian announced its intention of acquiring two One-Eleven 400s and two Series 500s later to supplement its ex-BEA Viscount 701s and 'Pionair' class DC-3s; no order was actually placed but Autair's Series 416s were acquired when these

came on to the market, G-AWBL being delivered a year after the others, on 15 February 1971. By this time Cambrian, along with Northeast Airlines (the former BKS Air Transport), had both been wholly-owned subsidiaries of British Air Services, in which BEA had a 70% interest, since November 1967; BEA had first acquired a holding in Cambrian of 33⅓% in 1958. With the formation of British Airways on 1 September 1972 by the merger of BOAC and BEA and their associated companies, Cambrian became known as British Airways – Cambrian and was later, with its One-Elevens, completely integrated into British Airways Regional Division, losing its separate identity.

Cambrian's One-Elevens officially began services on 3 April 1970, although some scheduled flights were operated before this; they flew the London-Liverpool route and also some inclusive tour flights from Bristol to Palma in Majorca, while one was also leased to BEA for use on its routes to Dublin during the 1970 season. Cambrian's One-Elevens were joined in British Airways Regional Division service by three more acquired late in 1973: the ex-Channel Series 408 G-BBMG (formerly G-AWEJ), delivered on 5 September that year and now named *County of Gloucestershire*, and two ex-American Airlines Series 401s, G-BBMF (previously VP-BDI of Bahamasair and N5032) and G-BBME (previously G-AZMI of Orientair Ltd and N5026). The latter had been delivered to Hurn on 29 January 1972 for operation by Orientair on inclusive tour flights from West Berlin for the German tour operator GUT, but this venture fell

Above:
Autair International Airways Ltd, which became Court Line (Aviation) Ltd on 1 January 1970, used four One-Eleven 416s on European inclusive tour charters. G-AVOF *Halcyon Breeze* seen here was the second of these, and was delivered on 19 March 1968.

through and G-AZMI was put into storage shortly afterwards; it was later registered G-16-19 before becoming G-BBME. The two Series 401s were used on Channel Island routes, G-BBME being named *County of Shropshire* in 1983 and G-BBMF *County of Worcestershire*; Series 408 G-BBMG was used on the Scottish routes, while the other ex-Channel and Cambrian Series 408, G-AVGP, was named *County of Nottinghamshire*.

The fourth ex-Autair One-Eleven 416, G-AWXJ *Halcyon Sun*, unlike its sisters that went to Cambrian and then BA Regional Division, had a rather more varied career after disposal by Autair. It returned to BAC and was resold in June 1970 to Aeroleasing of Geneva as HB-ITK but this deal fell through; it was restored to BAC on 19 August that year, and was demonstrated to Nigeria Airways executives at Gatwick on the 26th. It was later refurbished as an executive transport for Mr Robin Loh of Singapore, being handed over to him at Hurn as 9V-BEF on 3 November 1971; Mr Loh was chairman of the Robin Group of companies in Singapore and Hong Kong. It was leased to Air Siam from May 1972 to February 1973 to enable that airline, after a spell of heavy losses, to resume operations between Bangkok and Hong Kong. It was then leased again to Pelita Air Service PT, which operated the aircraft of Indonesia's state-owned oil company Pertamina, as PK-PJC from April to 15 May 1973, and again in 1974-75. Pelita sub-leased it to the Indonesian domestic carrier Merpati Nusantara Airlines to operate services from Denpasar on the island of Bali to Darwin for passengers from Australia visiting the beautiful holiday island; Merpati had previously leased One-Eleven 401 N5032 for a three-month trial period over its routes from 11 August 1971, but had decided that the time was not then ripe to order jets. After its last lease to Pertamina in 1979, PK-PJC was flown back to Hurn from Djakarta on 4 June that year to become G-16-24 and to be restored as G-CBIA for use by British Island Airways.

Dan-Air Services Ltd, unlike the other major British independent One-Eleven operators, built up its fleet of the type entirely from second-hand examples, acquiring two Series 401s, N5041 and N5044, from American Airlines, these becoming G-AXCP and G-AXCK respectively, and being delivered to Dan-Air's London Gatwick main base in March 1969. These were later joined by ex-Bavaria Series 414 D-ANDY which became G-AZED and was delivered on 21 December 1971. The One-Elevens shared with Dan-Air's Comets and Boeing 727s the operation of charter and IT flights from English provincial cities to continental and Mediterranean holiday resorts. As more Boeing 727s were acquired, G-AXCK was sold to Westinghouse Electric as N164W as an executive transport, being delivered on 3 February 1983; G-AXCP was wet-leased to British Midland Airways from 25 October 1982 to 10 January 1983.

One of the last airlines orders for the One-Eleven 400 was for six Series 424s for the Rumanian state airline TAROM placed through the state export/import agency Technoimport and announced on 26 February 1968. This was an important order for two reasons: it marked the first sales breakthrough of a British jet airliner into the Eastern bloc countries (although the Yugoslav airline JAT had put the Sud Caravelle 6N into service in January 1963), and it was linked to an agreement between Britten-Norman and the Rumanian Government for assembly of the Islander light transport in Rumania and its resale all over the world through Britten-Norman and its distributors; the Islander deal was to offset the cost of the One-Eleven 424s, which was some £9million.

TAROM's choice was made after an evaluation of airliners from the Soviet Union, France and the USA, and it led seven years later to a repeat order for five One-Eleven 525s and the May 1977 agreement for licence production of the One-Eleven in Rumania and the transfer of associated technology. The Rumanian order for Series 424s was one manifestation of an increasingly independent line the country's leaders were taking, away from the Kremlin; President Ceauşescu had played host to Marshal Tito and President Nixon during 1969, had begun to develop relations with China, and the previous year had stood with Tito against the Warsaw Pact countries' invasion of Czechoslovakia to stamp out Alexander Dubcek's more liberal version of Communist rule. With growing independence, tourism from Western Europe was encouraged, especially to the Black Sea holiday resorts, and in this TAROM's One-Elevens played their part.

The Series 424s were registered YR-BCA to YR-BCF, and the first YR-BCA, left Hurn for Bucharest on 14 June 1968, followed by YR-BCB on 17 December that year. The first one was soon flying 21 scheduled services a week as well as charter flights, linking Bucharest to Vienna, Zurich, Rome, Frankfurt, Brussels and London. Later Madrid, Paris, Amsterdam, Sofia, Budapest, Prague, Berlin and Copenhagen were served by the One-Eleven 424s which also expanded TAROM's routes eastward to Beirut, Tel Aviv and Cairo through Athens, Istanbul and Nicosia, as well as linking the Rumanian capital to Moscow non-stop and to Algiers via Zurich. A seventh One-Eleven, Series 401 YR-BCG (ex-N5035) was acquired from American Airlines and delivered on 20 June 1972, and was followed that August by Series 402 YR-BCH, originally destined for Philippine Air Lines and later operated by TAE of Spain as EC-BQF; TAROM had also used the Series 409 G-AXBB on lease from BAC from May to August 1969, prior to its delivery to LACSA of Costa Rica as TI-1055C. In 1975 TAROM formed a charter subsidiary known as Linii Aeriene Romane for charter flights to the Black Sea holiday resorts; this started operations in December that year with two of the One-Eleven 424s, followed by a third later; these were YR-BCC, named *Bacau*, YR-BCD and YR-BCF.

One-Eleven 400s had already proved themselves in Central America in service with TACA International, LACSA of Costa Rica, LANICA and TAN Airlines of Honduras. So it was not surprising when Bahamas Airways Ltd leased two 74-passenger Series 432s from BAC, which were first flown with the Class B registrations G-16-5 and G-16-14, becoming VP-BCY and VP-BCZ respectively, the former being delivered on 11 November 1968 and the latter on 4 December. They started services between Nassau and Miami, later between Miami and Freeport and from April 1970 from Nassau to Freeport. The airline had long been a financial loss-maker, in spite of serving a wealthy and popular holiday resort area just off Florida; Bahamas Airways' routes served the Turks and Caicos Islands at the south of the Bahamas island chain, as well as linking the capital of Nassau and Freeport, known for its casinos, to Miami, Fort Lauderdale and West Palm Beach.

In October 1968 BOAC had sold 85% of its holding in Bahamas Airways, which had been a wholly-owned subsidiary since 1949, to the great Hong Kong trading group of John Swire & Sons Ltd, which amongst other interests controlled the Hong Kong airline Cathay Pacific Airways Ltd. But neither the group's commercial skills nor the introduction of One-Elevens was sufficient to save Bahamas Airways, which went into liquidation on 9 October 1970. Two basic reasons seem to account

for the airline's long history of losses and eventual demise: first, the sheer intensity of the competition from larger US airlines such as Pan American and Eastern operating larger, more modern aircraft into Nassau from Miami and elsewhere, and secondly, the fact that Bahamas had always been a short-haul inter-island operator with no long-haul routes to major cities such as New York, Toronto, Chicago or London. Had One-Elevens been introduced earlier, and long-haul routes been awarded, it might have been a different story, although the BAC jets' introduction had been marked by big traffic increases. The two Series 432s were returned to BAC on 12 August 1969 when the first pair of Bahamas' One-Eleven 517s were delivered, VP-BCY becoming G-AXOX and VP-BCZ became G-AXMU. Bahamas also leased the ex-British Eagle Series 301 G-ATPK as VP-BCP from March 1970, this being sold to Laker Airways after its return from lease.

Bahamas Airways was succeeded by Bahamas-air Holdings Ltd, formed early in 1973 as the State-backed national airline and designated flag carrier of the Bahamas by the merger of two other Bahamian operators, Out Island Airways Ltd and Flamingo Airlines Ltd. Operations began in June 1973, a month before the Bahamas gained their independence from British rule, and like its predecessor, Bahamasair chose One-Elevens as first-line equipment, operating four ex-American Series 401s. Flamingo Airlines had also operated a One-Eleven 203 on lease from Braniff for a time, but this had been replaced by two Lockheed Electra turboprops. Bahamasair's first One-Eleven 401, VP-BDI, was formerly N5032 and had recently returned from lease to LANICA as AN-BHN; it was put on to the Nassau-Miami route but was fairly soon sold to British Airways Regional Division as G-BBMF, being delivered through Keflavik to Hurn on 18 December 1973.

It was followed in Bahamasair service by Series 401s VP-BDJ (ex-N5043), VP-BDN (ex-N5022) and VP-BDP (ex-N5023), these being re-registered C6-BDJ, C6-BDN and C6-BDP in April 1975 when the new Bahamas registration prefix came into effect. They were used mainly on the 184-mile Nassau-Miami and 130-mile Nassau-Freeport routes, with scheduled block times of only 45 and 30min respectively, and while the 79-passenger One-Elevens were more economical over such

short sectors than Eastern's Boeing 727s and TriStars that competed against them on the Miami run, they could lose in passenger appeal against the larger aircraft. In October 1975 a new One-Eleven route from Nassau to Port-au-Prince (Haiti) was inaugurated, but this is no longer operated. In 1976 C6-BDN became N5022 again with Dresser Industries and, from October that year, with the Garrett Corp. It has now been sold to Personal Way Aviation Inc. C6-BDJ and C6-BDP were both withdrawn from service by August 1981, being replaced by three Boeing 737-200s.

In the summer of 1984 C6-BDJ and C6-BDP were sold through the Beech Aircraft Corp to Cascade Airways Inc of Spokane, Washington, becoming N218CA and N217CA respectively; shortly after Cascade acquired on lease three of the ex-BUA Series 201s flown by Pacific Express, these being N102EX, N103EX and N106EX. The One-Elevens fly Cascade's network of commuter routes linking places in Washington to the neighbouring states of Oregon, Idaho and Montana, and over the Canadian border to Calgary, Alberta; the jets are supplemented by HS.748 turboprops, Beech 1900s, Swearingen Metro IIIs and Bandeirantes.

The two ex-Bahamas Airways One-Eleven 432s were acquired by Gulf Aviation Co Ltd of Bahrain (Gulf Air), the order for these two being announced on 29 July 1969. The first, G-AXOX, was delivered in January 1970, and was soon operating frequent flights from Bahrain to Doha in Qatar, to Abu Dhabi, Dubai and Sharjah in what was then Trucial Oman, and Muscat (Muscat and Oman), as well as to Dhahran (Saudi Arabia) and Kuwait. Services to Shiraz in Iran began in December 1970 and, with the delivery of the second Series 432, G-AXMU, on 3 November 1971, One-Eleven services to Karachi and Bombay started in January 1972, these doubling in frequency from November that year.

Britain's withdrawal from the Gulf in January

Above:
**Formerly PK-PJC and Mr Robin Loh's executive 9V-BEF, the
ex-Autair One-Eleven 416 G-CBIA was one of four acquired
by British Island Airways – BIA – for inclusive tour
operations from Gatwick to holiday resorts in Europe and
the Mediterranean.**

1972 led to the former BOAC holding of 25% in Gulf
Aviation through BOAC Associated Companies
being relinquished, and from 1 April 1974 the
airline was owned equally by the Gulf states of
Bahrain, Oman, Qatar and the United Arab
Emirates, of which Abu Dhabi, Dubai and Sharjah
were the most important; the name Gulf Air and a
new livery had been adopted early in 1973 for
marketing purposes. A third One-Eleven, Series
409 G-AXBB that had served with LACSA of Costa
Rica as TI-1055C and was restored to the British
register on 24 January 1974, joined Gulf Air's fleet
shortly after, and in October 1975 all three were
re-registered in the Sultanate of Oman. G-AXMU
became A40-BU, G-AXOX was A40-BX and
G-AXBB became A40-BB, while Series 413 D-ALLI
was leased from Bavaria about this time until April
1977, but flew under its German registration. The
first of five Boeing 737-2P6s was delivered to Gulf
Air in June 1977 and the three One-Eleven 432s
returned to the British register on 22 June 1978, all
being sold to British Island Airways.

This last airline, a former associate of British
United under the British & Commonwealth
Shipping Group, which remained with that Group
after the BUA/Caledonian merger of November
1970, acquired the three ex-Gulf Air One-Elevens
and the ex-Autair Series 416 G-CBIA (formerly
PK-PJC and the executive 9V-BEF) for use on
inclusive tour charters from London Gatwick to
European and Mediterranean holiday resorts. The
three Gulf Air One-Elevens were refurbished at
Hurn for BIA under a £1.5million contract, the first,
G-AXBB, being delivered on 13 December 1978 as
Island Envoy, being followed by G-AXOX on 6

January 1979 as *Island Endeavour* and G-AXMU on
9 February as *Island Esprit*. On 16 January 1980
British Island Airways merged with Air Anglia,
BIA/Air West (formerly Air Westward) and Air
Wales, three other airlines in the British &
Commonwealth Shipping Group Ltd, to form Air
UK; BIA's four One-Elevens joined the Air UK fleet,
being used, as they had been with BIA, entirely on
inclusive tour flights from Gatwick. Air UK's
scheduled services served 33 different airports, of
which 23 are within the UK, and were operated by
Fokker F.28 Fellowships, F.27 Friendships, Handley
Page Heralds and Embraer Bandeirantes.

In 1982 Air UK's parent company, British &
Commonwealth, revived the name British Island
Airways to cover its One-Eleven inclusive tour
operations, the first such IT service under the new
BIA name being operated out of Gatwick on 1 April;
the new BIA was now a separate and totally
independent airline under the new ownership of a
group of businessmen including Mr Peter Villa, Air
UK's then managing director. The four
One-Elevens were later joined in mid-1983 by the
ex-Autair Series 416 G-AVOF after a spell with Air
Manchester Ltd as G-BMAN; the other Series 416
G-CBIA was now named *Island Ensign*. Series 432
G-AXMU was leased to Air Cymru from April to
November 1984, and then to Virgin Atlantic
Airways for the latter's London Gatwick to
Maastricht route.

Also formed early in 1982 to operate inclusive
tour services, this time from Manchester, was Air
Manchester Ltd, whose founder was Sureway
Holidays. It started with the two ex-Autair and
Cambrian One-Eleven 416s G-AVOE and G-AVOF
acquired from British Airways Regional Division,
the first being re-registered G-SURE after Air
Manchester's parent company, and being delivered
on 18 May 1982, and the second, after a spell as
G-16-32, becoming G-BMAN and being delivered in
September. Initial holiday destinations for Air

Manchester included Palma, Ibiza, Barcelona, Alicante and Malaga in Spain, Faro in Portugal and Nice in France. British Air Ferries provided technical assistance for the One-Elevens, and G-SURE was leased to them for passenger charters in September 1982, but was flown to Lasham for storage by Dan-Air on 21 January 1983; it was restored to Dan-Air as G-AVOE and put back into service in May. G-BMAN was returned to British Aerospace as G-AVOF on 18 March 1983 and later leased to the new British Island Airways in May 1983.

The two Series 416s G-AVOE and G-AVOF were sold early in 1984 to US commuter airline Britt Airways Inc of Danville, Illinois, becoming N390BA and N492BA respectively; the former was delivered through Keflavik on 23 June that year. The One-Elevens fly Britt's commuter routes linking places in Illinois and Indiana, and also serving Paducah (Kentucky), Memphis (Tennessee), St Louis and Cape Girardeau (Missouri) and Burlington (Iowa). They are supplemented by Fairchild FH-227 and F-27J turboprops, Swearingen Metro IIs and Beech 99s.

Top:
On 16 January 1980 BIA merged with three other British domestic airlines to form Air UK, and G-CBIA was the first jet to appear in the new airline's striking new colour scheme of blue all over, with white and red fuselage flash and 'UK' in red. *Air UK*

Left:
G-SURE, formerly Autair's G-AVOE, was one of two One-Eleven 416s acquired by Air Manchester Ltd in 1982 to operate inclusive tours from that city. G-SURE took its registration from the airline's parent company Sureway Holidays. *D. Goodwin via J. M. G. Gradidge*

Below left:
Saudi Arabia is now the largest user of executive One-Elevens outside the USA, and HZ-MFI seen here is one Series 400 on the Saudi register. *D. Spurgeon via J. M. G. Gradidge*

65

The 475 and Rumanian Production

Last version of the One-Eleven to go into production was the Series 475, intended for what may be termed the 'country bus' type routes, especially in the less developed countries, away from the main centres of population and where difficult combinations of temperature and altitude might often be encountered. The Series 475, announced in January 1970, combined the fuselage and passenger accommodation of the Series 400 with the extended span wings and more powerful Spey 512-14DW turbofans of 12,550lb st (maximum take-off) as fitted to the Series 500, developed for European inclusive-tour operations. The letters DW in this engine designation signified Developed Wet, a reference to the water injection system fitted to restore power under 'hot and high' conditions, and later on hush kits could also be fitted if the customer so desired. Fitting the Series 500's powerplants and wing, with its new leading edge profile with more camber and a larger nose radius to increase the maximum lift coefficient, to the Series 400 fuselage gave the 475 the highest thrust-to-weight ratio of any One-Eleven, with correspondingly brisk take-off and climb out performance.

To permit operations into secondary airfields with low strength unpaved or gravel runways with a poorer grade surface than usual, the landing gear was fitted with larger diameter low-pressure tyres; the larger diameter of the mainwheels with these tyres fitted (44in instead of 40in) necessitated an enlarged and revised main wheel bay, actuation jacks, wheel doors and underbelly fairing, and a 3.8in increase in spacing between the centres of each pair of wheels. Mainwheel tyre pressure of the 475 was 81lb/sq in at a maximum take-off weight of 92,000lb compared with 141lb/sq in for the Series 400 at a maximum weight of 87,000lb. More powerful heavy duty hydraulic disc brakes very similar to the Series 500's were also fitted.

The Series 400/500 development aircraft, G-ASYD, was modified from its previous configuration as the Series 500 prototype to serve

Below right:
Compania de Aviacion Faucett SA used its two One-Eleven 476s on Peruvian domestic routes, operating out of some very high altitude Andean airports.

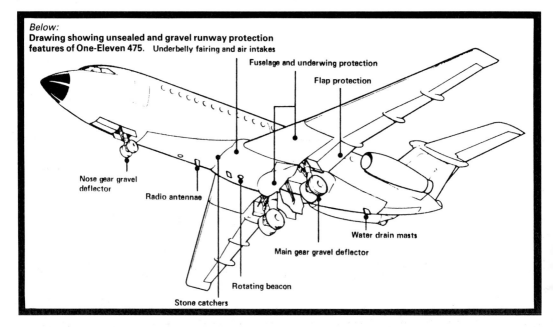

Below:
Drawing showing unsealed and gravel runway protection features of One-Eleven 475. Underbelly fairing and air intakes

Fuselage and underwing protection

Flap protection

Nose gear gravel deflector

Radio antennae

Water drain masts

Main gear gravel deflector

Rotating beacon

Stone catchers

as the Series 475 prototype. This conversion started in May 1970, after initial checks into operating on to gravel runways had been completed, and G-ASYD first flew in its Series 475 form on 27 August 1970. The flight test and certification programme of the 475 went exactly to schedule, and gravel runway trials with G-ASYD proved to be very satisfactory, first at Wisley and later at a special gravel runway at Waterbeach. To operate from this sort of runway only simple deflector places were necessary, fitted between each pair of nose and main wheels, plus the application of protective paint or fibre glass on the forward and centre part of the fuselage underside and the inner wing; the flaps are coated in fibre glass for extra protection. In addition some of the more fragile items on the Series 475 such as radio aerials or anti-collision beacons have been suitably protected, and several stone catchers are positioned on the under fuselage to protect both these and the engine intakes from stone impact or ingestion. This degree of protection was also suitable for unprepared runway surfaces of grass or coral.

First customer for the 475 was the Peruvian airline Compania de Aviacion Faucett SA, which ordered one Series 476EZ in June 1970 and one more later. The first production aircraft G-AYUW (previously G-16-17) made its maiden flight on 5 April 1971, three weeks ahead of schedule, and left on delivery to Faucett at Lima on 26 July, becoming OB-R-953. The second for Faucett, G-AZUK (formerly G-16-16) made an extensive demonstration tour of South America during 1972 during which 21 airfields were visited, 10 of which had never been flown into by a jet before; G-AZUK later became OB-R-1080 in Faucett service. The airline used the One-Elevens on its domestic routes, operating out of such very high altitude airports as Cuzco at 10,500ft, serving one of the centres of the old Inca civilisation; this is the sort of airport where the 475's high thrust-to-weight ratio really comes into its own.

Unlike most old-established Latin American airlines Faucett had always concentrated on developing domestic routes rather than international ones ever since its formation by an American, Elmer J. Faucett, on 15 September 1928. In its earliest days it used two Stinson Detroiter high wing monoplanes and the airline later designed and built in its own workshops an eight-passenger high wing monoplane known as the Faucett-Stinson F.19, which first flew on 20 September 1934. Thirty F.19s were built by Faucett up to 1947, including six for the Peruvian Government, and a few were fitted with floats; the F.19 remained in service until mid-1964 and Faucett was almost unique among airlines in operating aircraft of its own manufacture. After the war Faucett acquired DC-3s and four DC-4s for the domestic routes; the first DC-6B joined the fleet in 1960 and a Boeing 727-63 was delivered on 9 April 1968, followed by a 727-51C some time later. By 1978 One-Eleven 523 OB-R-1137 had been acquired from Transbrasil SA to supplement the two Series 476s, this being the former PP-SDT which had previously been G-AXLL of British Midland. Of the first two, OB-R-953 flew its last service on 31 December 1982 while OB-R-1080 was withdrawn from use in June 1982; the Series 523, OB-R-1137,

was flown over to Filton in October 1983, after a period in storage, for refurbishing and resale. It joined British Caledonian's fleet as G-AXLL early in 1984.

Next customer after Faucett was Air Pacific Ltd, the former Fiji Airways, which ordered one Series 479 late in 1970 and announced the purchase of a second in September 1972. The first, DQ-FBQ, left Hurn on delivery via Brindisi on 4 March 1972 and the second, DQ-FBV, followed on 14 August 1973. The first One-Eleven service was flown on 2 April 1972 on the route from Nadi International Airport serving the capital, Suva, to Port Moresby in New Guinea via Port Vila in the New Hebrides Islands and Honiara in the Solomon Islands. On 1 June 1973 a new service from Nadi to Brisbane was inaugurated via Port Vila in the New Hebrides and Honiara, but towards the end of that year Air Pacific was in a rather poor shape financially because a rise in fuel prices and labour costs had coincided with a traffic recession. The full capacity of the One-Elevens could not be utilised partly because the traffic rights for new regional routes for which they had been bought had not yet all been granted, and partly because, mainly through lack of capital, the process of sealing and upgrading airport runways in the region even to the less demanding jet standards of the One-Eleven 479 was not yet complete.

The airline was recapitalised in August 1974 and to solve the problem of One-Eleven over-capacity Series 479 DQ-FBQ was leased to Air Malawi from 9 July 1974 to 16 November 1975, becoming 7Q-YKG. The remaining One-Eleven opened a new

route from Nadi to Auckland, New Zealand via Tongatapu on Tonga in the Friendly Isles, and since 1 July 1975 it operated an alternative routeing on the Nadi-Brisbane service via Noumea in New Caledonia instead of Honiara. Port Moresby in new Guinea is no longer served, the Honiara-Port Moresby sector having been taken over by Air Niugini F.27 Friendships in July 1975.

As related in the previous chapter, Air Pacific acquired One-Eleven 408 D-ALLI, formerly G-AWGG of Channel Airways, from Bavaria Fluggesellschaft as DQ-FCR, this being delivered via Bahrain on 26 June 1978. It was grounded by corrosion late in 1980 and withdrawn from use, a Boeing 737-200 being leased from Air New Zealand to replace it; a new Boeing 737-2X2 has now been delivered, Air Pacific being the 100th customer for the type. Airport improvements now allowed the One-Elevens as well as the 737 to operate some of the flights over the 25min sector between Suva, the capital, and Nadi International Airport, supplementing the Hawker-Siddeley HS.748 turboprops and now Bandeirantes used on this route. The two One-Elevens were flown back to Gatwick in March 1984 and acquired by the Ministry of Defence, being given RAF serials. DQ-FBV is now ZE432 with the Empire Test Pilots' School and DQ-FBQ serves the RAE, Bedford, as ZE433.

Next airline customer after Air Pacific was Air Malawi Ltd, national airline of the country formerly known as Nyasaland in colonial days; this had been formed in March 1964 as a wholly-owned subsidiary of the old Central African Airways Corp but had become an entirely separate national carrier in September 1967 following Rhodesia's UDI. Air Malawi announced an order for one One-Eleven 489 in September 1971 to replace the Series 207 previously leased from Zambia Airways in November 1970. The Series 489 was delivered as 7Q-YKF on 23 February 1972, and went into service on routes from Blantyre, the capital, to

Above:
Above:
The Series 475 prototype G-ASYD was converted into the One-Eleven 670, a variant intended as a YS-11 turboprop replacement for the Japanese domestic airlines. This had 20in wing-tip extensions, a revised leading edge profile and wide-choard Fowler-type flaps.

Johannesburg, Nairobi (Kenya) and Lusaka in Zambia, as well as to Dar es Salaam in Tanzania. The first One-Eleven, which seated 84 passengers, was supplemented by Series 479 7Q-YKG (formerly DQ-FBQ) on lease from Air Pacific during 1974-75, and in April 1975 the One-Elevens took over the route from Blantyre to Mauritius previously operated by Air Malawi's two Viscount 700s, and there was also a service from Blantyre to the Seychelles, which is no longer operated. British Caledonian leased One-Eleven 501 G-AXJM *Isle of Islay* to Air Malawi as 7Q-YKI from 3 to 17 December 1977, and in October 1979 leased Series 530 G-AZMF *Isle of Raasay*, which became 7Q-YKJ and was returned for a further lease to British Airways the following April. Air Malawi then acquired One-Eleven 524 D-AMAT from Hapag Lloyd, this becoming 7Q-YKK and being delivered from Frankfurt on 30 October 1980.

In the end the Faucett, Air Pacific and Air Malawi orders were to be the only airline ones for the Series 475, and that more were not sold – only nine were built in all, plus two more left unsold when the One-Eleven production line at Hurn closed down in 1982 – can probably be attributed mainly to the fuel price rises and onset of recession that followed the 1973 Arab-Israeli war. This caused airlines, especially in the developing countries, which might have considered ordering the Series 475, to take a fresh look at turboprops or to postpone any expansion of their domestic routes. The next order for this variant, in mid-1974, was for three Series 475EZ military freighters for the Sultan of Oman's Air Force, this Sultanate having been

formed in August 1970 from Muscat and Oman. This strategically important Sultanate, on the 'horn' of Arabia and at the entrance to the Persian (or Arabian) Gulf, had started oil production as recently as 1967, and had in about three years grown 15 times richer as a result, but it also faced the problems of Chinese-backed rebels in Dhofar in the far south of the territory. It was against this threat that the small but well-equipped Omani Air Force, in which seconded RAF personnel played an important part, had seen action, and for which the One-Elevens were to be the longer range transports.

They differed from previous One-Elevens in having a quick-change passenger/freight interior, which could carry typically 54 passengers and about five tons of freight (or six containers), and a hydraulically-powered upward-opening forward freight door in the port side measuring 10ft 0in × 6ft 1in. Although a military freighter version of the Series 300 with a very similar freight door had been announced in 1963, along with several other military variants, the Omani 475s were the first actually to have such a door installed, and this could in fact have been fitted retrospectively or during initial manufacture to any other version of the One-Eleven if a customer so desired. Both the door and the associated cargo handling system were of generally similar design to those on the East African Airways Super VC10s, and an optional feature of the freight door was that it could be opened nearly to the vertical if desired for easier loading by a crane. A quickly removable freight floor overlay is featured, and the inner surface of the freight door matches the basic cabin interior, so that it becomes barely discernible when passengers are carried. Containers and 108in × 88in pallets to international standards can be carried.

The first Omani 475 freighter, bearing the serial 1001, made its maiden flight on 21 November 1974, and was delivered on 28 December. The second, serialled 1002, was delivered on 29 January 1975 and the third, with the serial 1003, was delivered in October that year. Shortly after, on 22-23 November, 1003 was damaged by an oxygen bottle fire and was shipped back the following May for repair and a rebuild at Hurn; just before this fire occurred the freight doors of both 1001 and 1003 had been modified slightly. Later, all three were given new serials, 1001 becoming 551, 1002 changing to 552 and 1003 now being 553. The first of these, 551, was refitted as a VIP/executive transport for the Royal Flight, with long range tankage, during the summer of 1983; the other two One-Elevens previously equipped No 4 Squadron although the Air Force's transports are now allocated to different squadrons as required.

Although the freight door and freighter interior were available to civil operators, no airline used the One-Eleven in the freighter role largely because virtually all the European operators of the type used them almost exclusively for the holiday inclusive tour charter traffic, rather than for scheduled services where all-freight or mixed passenger/freight operations could maintain the utilisation and revenue earned during off-peak and out of season traffic periods. BEA, probably the biggest potential customer for a freighter One-Eleven, chose instead to use Argosy 222s for freighting during 1965-70 and to follow these with an all-freight conversion of the Vanguard known as the V.953C Merchantman. In the United States, too, One-Elevens were ordered by airlines, especially the local service carriers, that were interested in passengers rather than freight, and whose freighter needs were filled by cargo conversions of larger types. The last Series 475 to be delivered to a

customer was the first executive one; this was HZ-MAM for Mr Mouaffak Al Midani, which was handed over at Hurn on 11 May 1978 and was then flown out to Los Angeles to complete its fitting out as an executive transport. It joined several other ex-airline corporate One-Elevens (mostly ex-American Airlines Series 401s) on the Saudi register. The two left unsold when production at Hurn ceased were designated Series 492GM and registered to British Aerospace as G-BLDH and G-BLHD. They both made their first flights on 2 February 1984.

Meanwhile a developed variant of the Series 475, the One-Eleven 670, had been offered to Japanese domestic airlines in 1976 as a replacement for the twin-Dart NAMC YS-11 turboprop, a 60-passenger airliner of which 182 were built; this was used by some of the more important Japanese domestic carriers such as Toa Domestic Airlines and All Nippon, and had achieved some important export orders in South America and the USA. The One-Eleven 670 featured a further improved wing with extended span in the shape of 20in wing tip extensions, a revised leading edge profile and wider-chord Fowler-type flaps to give the requisite 4,000ft runway capability for Japanese requirements; other engineering and interior changes were also incorporated. The Series 475 prototype made a demonstration tour of Japan in October 1976, and proved its ability to operate into the many 1,200m (4,000ft) runways in that country used by YS-11s. There was some discussion with the Japanese aircraft industry about possible Japanese participation in Series 475 production and development in the event of an order being placed by one of their airlines; Toa Domestic Airlines and All Nippon Airways at that time still

operated about 60 YS-11s between them, so the potential market was there. In 1977 the Series 475 prototype G-ASYD was converted to serve as the Series 670 development aircraft, and first flew in this form on 13 September that year. But in the end All Nippon continued to use Boeing 737-200s for its short haul jet services, and Toa Domestic stuck to its DC-9 Series 41s and 80s and still has 35 YS-11As; All Nippon continues to operate 19 of the Japanese turboprops.

Rumanian Production

The Rumanian state airiine TAROM had followed its 1968 order for six One-Eleven 424s with another for five Series 525s in the spring of 1975, and this led to the agreement concluded on 28 May 1977 between BAC and the Grupul Aeronautic Bucuresti for the licence production of the One-Eleven 500 in Rumania and the transfer of associated technology. This agreement was concluded in a finalised form by British Aerospace at Filton on 15 June 1978 during a visit to the factory by the Rumanian President, and it is much wider in scope than the conventional arrangements for licence production of an aircraft in a foreign country, covering as it does various counter-trade arrangements by British Aerospace on behalf of Rumanian products, type certification of Rumanian-built One-Elevens locally by the country's DAvC airworthiness authority and the training of Rumanian test pilots and engineers for their own One-Eleven flight testing, as well as Rumanian personnel in production techniques. All these aspects were additional to the transfer of technology to help build up a self-sufficient aircraft industry, to which the Rumanian Government attached a high priority, and the One-Eleven agreement is valued in excess of £150million. It followed on naturally from the earlier agreement for the manufacture of the Britten-Norman Islander in Rumania and its resale all over the world through Britten-Norman and its distributors. Negotiations for the One-Eleven agreement began in 1976 and were protracted, not so much because of any technical problems but because of the need to devise financial arrangements acceptable to both sides, since Rumania had to pay for Western imports in hard currency that usually had to be earned from exports.

This accounts for the various counter-trade arrangements in which British Aerospace helps to identify buyers for a wide range of Rumanian products in markets throughout the world, and in the aviation field this has led to BAe arranging for Slingsby Engineering Ltd to distribute the Rumanian IS-28 and IS-29 high performance sailplanes and the IS-28M motor glider in this country, while BAe was also instrumental in bringing Pilatus and the Rumanians together when the Swiss company took over Britten-Norman in 1979. Continuing Rumanian production of the Islander now forms part of the One-Eleven offset deal. By 1980 about 160 items had been covered in counter-trade deals, including a good many aviation products, while non-aviation deals have been made in the fields of steel, motor components, railway rolling stock and petrochemicals. These deals, and the British management of the whole contract, are the responsibility of ROMBAC as BAe's Rumanian specialist projects group at Hurn is known, and ROMBAC as BAe's Rumanian specialist projects group at Hurn is known, and ROMBAC is also assisting the Rumanians in type certification of their

Left:
The first of three complete British-built One-Eleven fuselages for Rumania being loaded into Aeromaritime Super Guppy F-BPPA in January 1980 for delivery to Bucharest.

71

One-Elevens and training for the Rumanian flight test programme.

About 80 One-Elevens are to be built over a period of 15 years at Baneasa, the manufacturing complex near Bucharest, under the terms of the agreement. The Rumanians have also taken a licence to assemble the Spey 512-14DW for their One-Elevens, which will have hush kits, a total of 225 of these engines being produced and tested over the same 15-year period; eventually half of the engine by value will be built in Rumania. To start the technology transfer education process, and to provide the Rumanians with pattern aircraft for their own production, two One-Eleven 525s and a series 487GK freighter built at Hurn were supplied to TAROM. The two Series 525s, YR-BCN and YR-BCO, were delivered on 16 January 1981 and 12 March 1982, YR-BCO being the last One-Eleven to be assembled at Hurn, and the Series 487GK, YR-BCR, was delivered on 28 July 1981. The first 22 Rumanian One-Elevens will embody UK-supplied structural components, parts and details on a progressively diminishing scale, so that after the 22nd aircraft the One-Elevens will be completely Rumanian-built, the technology transfer being scheduled for completion in seven stages by 1986. The first nine of the initial 22 will probably go to TAROM, and after the 22nd aircraft One-Elevens will be manufactured at the Baneasa plant, which was built for Interprinderea de Avioane Bucuresti (IAvB), at the rate of six a year, about half of these being for Rumanian domestic use and the rest for export markets.

The first Rumanian-built One-Eleven 560, YR-BRA, was rolled out on 27 August 1982 and first flew on 18 September, being fitted out to seat 104 passengers; the second, YR-BRB, was exhibited at the 1983 Paris Salon Internationale de L'Aéronautique et de l'Espace. YR-BRA received its Rumanian CofA on 17 December 1982, and was handed over to TAROM on 24 December. Meanwhile as Rumanian production built up, outsize freighter aircraft were used to fly large British-built components to Baneasa. The first of three complete fuselages delivered in 1980 was flown out by Aeromaritime Super Guppy F-BPPA in January, while a British Cargo Airlines Conroy CL-44-0 (the outsize freighter conversion of the Canadair CL-44D-4) carried wings and other major structural parts to Rumania, and TAROM Antonov AN-26 freighters flew out many of the smaller components in containers. BAe also supplied some conversion kits for Series 475 passenger and cargo variants (the Series 475 freighter is available for Rumanian production), as well as a range of assembly jigs and tools and other production items. In the opposite direction, the Rumanians had already been acting as subcontractors to British production several years before their first indigenously-build One-Eleven flew; as part of the offset deals that accompanied TAROM's One-Eleven 525 order they supplied the entire tailplane and elevator, rudder, wing leading edges, freight doors and the ventral airstairs for the Hurn One-Eleven line.

The ROMBAC One-Eleven programme is administered overall by CNIAR (the Central National Al Industrei Aeronautice Romane) which is the national centre of Rumania's aerospace industry, with the IAvB factory at Baneasa as the nominated prime factory and ICE-CNA (Interprinderea de Comert Exterior – Centrul National Aeronautic), which is the foreign trade company for Rumania's aircraft industry, handling all the business arrangements.

Below:
The second Rumanian-built One-Eleven 560 YR-BRB as displayed statically at the 1983 Paris Salon, with the words 'Manufactured by Interprinderea de Avioane Bucuresti – Rumania' below the cabin windows. It is that company which operates the Baneasa plant where Rumanian One-Elevens are built.

The One-Eleven 500

Definite plans for a stretched version of the One-Eleven were slower to mature than in the case of the Douglas DC-9 and Boeing 737, even though possible stretched versions had been the subject of studies by BAC since before the prototype first flew. This delay was due at least partly to the fact that the One-Eleven had to prove not just itself in airline service but the whole basic concept of the short-haul jet as an economically viable mode of transport. By contrast the DC-9 Series 30, the first major stretched variant of Douglas's short-haul jet, with a 15ft longer fuselage seating up to 115 passengers, was being designed late in 1964 before the prototype DC-9 first flew, so as to catch the big orders expected from Eastern and United. It featured more powerful JT8D-9 turbofans than the initial production DC-9 Series 10 and, as well as the longer fuselage and higher design weights, completely revised high lift devices for the wing, which now had full-span leading edge slats and triple-slotted instead of double-slotted flaps to maintain airfield performance at the higher weights; extended wing tips added 4ft to the span. The DC-9 Series 30 entered service first with Eastern in February 1967. The first stretched variant of Boeing's short-haul jet, the 737-200, was first ordered by United, which signed for 40, in April 1965 and this had a 6ft fuselage stretch, bringing passenger seating up to 119, or later up to 130 in high-density layouts. The 737-200 began services with United on 28 April 1968.

By contrast the One-Eleven, although the first of the three rival short-haul jets to fly and the first to begin airline services, was the last to be the subject of a firm order in its stretched form. It was not until BEA decided to order such a variant to replace Viscounts on its UK domestic and German internal routes that the go-ahead could be given, and initial studies with BEA began early in 1966. The One-Eleven 500 project was refined and substantially improved in the next few months and the final specification, agreed on in September 1966, bore little resemblance to the original proposals. On 27 January 1967 BEA signed a contract for 18 One-Eleven 510s plus six more on option and this order, worth £32million, was coupled to a Government contribution of £9million in launching aid to back One-Eleven 500 development. BEA's Series 510s were to seat 97 passengers and were scheduled to begin services on the German internal routes in the summer of 1968, also operating from London to Hanover and Berlin and from London to Manchester.

The basic Series 500 was designed to give the best economic performance on really short-haul routes of 150 to 400 miles; it has a 15% lower seat-mile cost than the Series 400 and is 25% larger. It has a 13ft 6in increase in fuselage length, this being made up of an 8ft 4in section forward of the wings and a 5ft 2in 'plug' aft of them, the total increase in length adding the equivalent of four more seat rows to the cabin space. There is now

Below:
The One-Eleven 500 prototype was converted from the Series 400 development aircraft G-ASYD by adding the lengthened fuselage inserts of the Series 500. It retained the lower-powered Spey 511-14s of the Series 400 and carried about 12,000lb of test instrumentation and equipment.

Below:
BEA Series 510 G-AVMT at Berlin's Tempelhof airport; BEA used its One-Elevens on routes linking major West German cities to Berlin, services from London to Berlin, Bremen, Dusseldorf and Hanover and on certain domestic and Irish routes.

Table 6 **One-Eleven 500 Weight Growth**				
One-Eleven 500	*Max take-off wt (lb)*	*Max land-ing wt (lb)*	*Max zero fuel wt (lb)*	*Max payload (lb)*
As originally specified, 1967	91,000	84,000	78,000	24,000
Series 510 for BEA, August 1968	92,483	85,980	–	24,000
With 109 IT seats and Spey 512-14DWs, early 1969	99,650	87,000	81,000	27,089
With 350gal aux fuel tank and up to 119 IT seats, August 1969	104,500	87,000	81,000	27,089

accommodation for 97-119 passengers, and at a seat pitch of 34in 99 can be accommodated in five-abreast rows; as before, a flight crew of two is the normal complement. The wing has a new leading edge profile with more camber and a larger nose radius to increase the maximum lift coefficient, and wing tip extensions increase the span by 5ft to cater for the higher design weights and improve the take-off performance. New and improved low drag flap track fairings are also featured but, unlike the DC-9 Series 30, it was not found necessary to introduce leading edge slats on the Series 500. To cater for the higher weights the main undercarriage is strengthened and heavier wing plank stringers are featured.

BEA's Series 510s were powered by 12,000lb st (maximum take-off) Spey 512-14 turbofans without water injection, this variant of the Spey already being Government-funded for BEA's Trident 2Es. But all subsequent Series 500s for other airlines were powered by the 12,550lb st (maximum take-off) Spey 512-14DW, this variant of the engine being specified for European inclusive tour operations, and the letter DW in the designation signified Developed Wet, meaning the water injection system for restoring power under 'hot and high' conditions. The combination of increased power and the extended wing tips means that, in spite of higher permitted operating weights, the Series 500 has a better airfield performance and can carry more payload than the Series 400. A larger capacity version of the same Garrett AiResearch auxiliary power unit in the tail cone is also featured.

The Series 500 aerodynamic prototype was converted from the Series 400 development aircraft G-ASYD, which was flown into Hurn on 4 February 1967 for the conversion process to start. By 28 April it was structurally complete, with the lengthened fuselage inserts in place, and adaptation of the aircraft systems followed, together with the installation of flight test instrumentation and associated equipment. Engine runs were made and completed on 22 June, the original lower-powered Spey 511-14s being fitted initially, these being standard on the Series 400. On 30 June six weeks ahead of the scheduled target date, G-ASYD took off at Hurn for a 74min first flight as the Series 500 with Brian Trubshaw, manager flight operations of the Weybridge and Filton Divisions of BAC, at the controls; take-off weight was 77,000lb and G-ASYD was flown at heights up to 25,000ft, while Mr Trubshaw was able to report that the aeroplane was entirely snag-free. G-ASYD carried 12,000lb of comprehensive test instrumentation and equipment to measure and record about 800 parameters simultaneously and continuously throughout flight. There were automatic cameras, 50-channel trace recorders and three magnetic tape recorders with

13 channels each. Flight tests with G-ASYD soon showed improved take-off and landing distances over those at first specified and in 1969 a further refined wing leading edge was test flown, and the take-off weight increased.

The first production aircraft, Series 510 G-AVMH for BEA, made its maiden flight on 7 February 1968, 10 weeks ahead of schedule, and Air Registration Board certification was granted on 15 August that year for BEA's Series 510s at a maximum take-off weight of 92,483lb, an increase over the 91,000lb originally specified. Deliveries to BEA began with G-AVMJ on 29 August 1968, more than a month ahead of schedule, and the first scheduled BEA service with the Series 510 was flown from Manchester on 17 November, although the type first started to earn revenue on non-scheduled services about two months before. One-Eleven 510s soon started operating the routes linking major German cities to Berlin, which BEA flew as the airline of one of the 'Occupying Powers'; Bremen, Bonn/Cologne, Dusseldorf, Frankfurt, Hamburg, Hanover, Munich and Stuttgart were all linked to Berlin by the Series 510s. They also flew direct services from London to Berlin, Bremen, Dusseldorf and Hanover, and from both Manchester and Glasgow to Berlin and Dusseldorf. The BAC jets enabled BEA to achieve a dramatic 35% traffic increase on the German internal routes. The One-Elevens also linked London to Manchester, Birmingham, Shannon and Dublin, as well as Manchester to Glasgow and Birmingham to Glasgow and Dublin.

BEA's aircraft were fitted with the Elliot Automation 2000 autopilot with an integral monitoring system for Category 2 autoland touch downs (100ft decision height and a quarter mile runway visual range); the autoland system also includes auto-throttles, a flare computer and a monitored radio altimeter. BEA's fleet was also fitted with the Decca Omnitrac moving map display, which proved very necessary for the extremely precise flying required in the 20-mile wide Berlin air corridors. Later the One-Elevens, now under British Airways ownership, were retrofitted with engine hush kits from 1979, and a repeat order for three, designated Series 539, was placed by BA late in 1978, these also having a 'wide body' look cabin interior as well as hush kits. These three were G-BGKE *County of West Midlands*, delivered on 22 February 1980, G-BGKF *County of Stafford*, delivered on 3 March and G-BGKG *County of Warwick* handed over on 18 August; the names were not actually given to this last trio until they had been in service for some time. British Airways also leased One-Eleven 537 5B-DAJ from Cyprus Airways as G-BFWN from 15 October 1978 to 28 April 1980, and One-Eleven 530 G-AZMF *Isle of Raasay* from British Caledonian after its return

from lease to Air Malawi as 7Q-YKJ on 24 April 1980.

Next customer after BEA was Caledonian Airways Ltd, which announced an order for three One-Eleven 509s on 4 March 1968, followed by British United Airways which contracted for five Series 501s a couple of months later. It was for charter operators like Caledonian that the more powerful version with Spey 512-14DW engines and a maximum weight of 99,650lb was developed, this being intended for the rapidly growing European inclusive tour holiday market, where many resorts around the Mediterranean, in North Africa and on the Black Sea were within a 1,000 to 1,500-mile radius of European traffic centres in the UK, Germany and Scandinavia. The first three of this developed version, which also offered an extended range made possible by the Series 500's wing refinements, were the Series 509s for Caledonian, G-AWWX, G-AWWY and G-AWWZ, which entered service as 109-seaters on the inclusive tour holiday routes in April 1969. The extended range allowed a full passenger payload to be carried on routes of up to 1,570 miles. British United's Series 501s, registered G-AWYR to G-AWYV, also seated 109 passengers, and on 30 November 1970 BUA merged with Caledonian to form Caledonian/BUA, later to be known, from 1 September 1972, as British Caledonian Airways. BUA had placed a repeat order for three Series 501s about four months after its original order, and these were delivered as G-AXJK, G-AXJL and G-AXJM in March 1970 in time for that summer's IT operations. The Caledonian/BUA One-Eleven 501s and 509s were named after Scottish islands from 1971, and were later refurbished with 'wide body'-look cabin interiors.

In August 1969 a further weight increase and yet more range were offered to prospective customers by the fitting of a supplementary 350Imp gal fuel tank in the aft end of the forward freight hold, this increasing the maximum weight to 104,500lb and enabling a maximum of 119 passengers to be carried for group charter and inclusive tour operations. Together with the extra fuel tankage and increased weight this variant featured several aerodynamic improvements, including a further refined wing leading edge, which was test flown on the Series 500 prototype G-ASYD. The first aircraft to feature all these improvements was the One-Eleven 515 D-ALAR, delivered on 30 May 1970 to the German charter operator Paninternational of Munich (or Panair, as it was also known until 31 December 1969), which took delivery of second and third Series 515s, D-ALAS and D-ALAT, soon after and a fourth, D-ALAQ, in March 1971.

Paninternational was a subsidiary of Paneuropa, a leading German tour operator, and its One-Elevens were used to fly charters and inclusive tour flights to the Canary Isles, the Mediterranean resorts and North Africa. But the airline ceased operations on 6 October 1971 and went into liquidation on 31 December that year, and of its One-Elevens D-ALAS was returned to BAC as G-AZPE, being delivered to Hurn on 18 March 1972, and leased to British Caledonian from 14 August to 18 October that year. D-ALAQ was disposed of to Germanair as D-AMAM in May 1972 after first becoming G-AZPZ, and was later restored to the British register nine years later when it was sold to Dan-Air Services. This was after service with Bavaria Flug, which had merged with Germanair on 1 January 1977 to form Bavaria Germanair Fluggesellschaft. Similarly D-ALAT became G-AZPY and then, in May 1972, D-AMAS of Germanair.

The frequency of leases, by B.Cal and other One-Eleven 500 operators, to other airlines often in

another continent and with quite different operating and climatic conditions, underlines the aircraft's essential versatility. B Cal's G-AXJK *Isle of Staffa* was leased to the Argentine operator Austral in 1975, while G-AWWY *Isle of Iona* was leased to Austral as LV-PSW in December 1973 for the peak summer (in the southern hemisphere) traffic, being restored to the British register on 7 February 1974. It was sold to Austral in October 1975 as LV-JNU, later becoming LV-LHT. G-AXJL *Isle of Mingulay* was sold to Philippine Air Lines late in 1976 as RP-C1188 and, as related in the previous chapter, G-AXJM *Isle of Islay* was leased to Air Malawi as 7Q-YKI in December 1977. Further sales by B.Cal were G-AWWX *Flagship Isle of Skye* and G-AXYD *Isle of Arran* (the fourth ordered by Caledonian) to Dan-Air Services Ltd, while G-AWWZ *Isle of Eriskay* was leased to Monarch Airlines of Luton from 14 November 1975, and later bought outright by that company. The Series 530 G-AZMF was leased to Air Malawi as 7Q-YKJ, but had also been chartered as PT-TYY to Transbrasil SA Linhas Aereas (formerly Sadia) from February to December 1974.

B.Cal also acquired several second-hand One-Eleven 500s; two ex-Bavaria Series 528s, D-ALFA *Jakob Fugger* and D-ANUE *Albrecht Durer*, were acquired as G-BJRT and G-BJRU, both being delivered on 29 October 1981, and the ex-Court Line Series 518 G-AYOP joined the fleet on 15 March 1973, being named *Isle of Hoy* and modified to Series 530 standard. The ex-Paninternational (or Panair) Series 515 G-AZPE (formerly D-ALAS) was leased from BAC for a time in 1972 while G-AWYS was undergoing repairs; it was returned on 18 October that year. Another Series 515, G-AZPZ (ex-D-AMAM) was acquired on long-term lease from Dan-Air on 1 March 1982, and was named *City of Glasgow*. Latest addition to the B.Cal fleet is Series 523 G-AXLL acquired from Faucett.

The One-Eleven 500 proved to be as popular with German inclusive tour operators as the Series 400 had been, and another German charter operator to become a customer was Germanair Bedarfsluftfahrt GmbH of Frankfurt, which ordered three Series 524s in mid-1969 plus one more later and then a further two. The first of these, D-AMIE, was delivered on 17 October 1969, and was followed by D-AMUR on 16 December that year, D-AMOR on 20 March 1970 and D-AMAT on 8 May 1971. Pending delivery of the first, the ex-LACSA One-Eleven 409 G-AXBB was leased from BAC in August 1969. It was early in 1971 that Josef Schörgruber became the major shareholder in Germanair, with an 80% financial interest, and since he already had a 26% holding in Bavaria Fluggesellschaft an eventual merger of these two charter and IT operators was logical. Schörgruber also controlled the investment company that owned the fleet of another German charter operator, Atlantis Airways, which operated DC-8 Series 63CFs and DC-8 Series 33s on worldwide passenger and cargo charters, as well as three DC-9 Series 32s. In addition to its One-Elevens Germanair also operated for a time the four Fokker F.28 Fellowships owned by the newly-formed charter airline Bonair based at Frankfurt.

Germanair used its 114-passenger One-Elevens on a wide-ranging network of inclusive tour holiday routes from West German cities to resorts in the Mediterranean and North Africa. The airline's chairman, Baron Christian von Kaltenborn-Stachau, in speaking of his airline's choice of the One-Eleven 500 said ' . . . in financing, operating cost efficiency, support and market acceptance (it) provides the best overall combination of factors for our type of jet operation.' This was a verdict that many other charter and inclusive tour operators in Europe would have endorsed because in 1969, in the UK alone, 1½ million IT holidaymakers were travelling to the sun by One-Eleven. After Paninternational went into liquidation at the end of 1971, two of its Series 515s, D-ALAQ and D-ALAT, were acquired by Germanair in May 1972, becoming D-AMAM and D-AMAS, as mentioned previously. Two of the Series 524s, D-AMIE and D-AMUR, were sold through BAC to Philippine Air Lines late in 1974, becoming RP-C1184 and RP-C1185 respectively, and when Germanair merged with Bavaria Fluggesellschaft on 1 January 1977 to form Bavaria Germanair Fluggesellschaft, the remaining Germanair One-Elevens D-AMAS, D-AMAT, D-AMAM and D-AMOR joined the Bavaria fleet.

Bavaria Flug had been a successful operator of One-Eleven 414s and its experience led to an order for two Series 528s, plus a third ordered late in 1971. The first of these, D-AMUC *Ludwig Thoma*, was delivered on 3 December 1970, followed by D-ALFA *Jakob Fugger* on 26 February 1971 and D-ANUE *Albrecht Durer* on 15 March 1972; the names were not applied until they had been in service for some time. These were used to provide more capacity on the holiday routes that the Series 414s had made so popular with the German travelling public, and after the merger with Germanair at the beginning of 1977 four of the latter's aircraft were taken over. At about this time Bavaria Germanair's One-Eleven 500s were fitted by National Aircraft Leasing of Los Angeles with an auxiliary fuel tank in the forward underfloor freight hold to give a further 600 nautical miles range for non-stop flights from Munich to the Canary Islands and Cairo. The first One-Eleven with this extra tankage flew non-stop from Gander, Newfoundland, to Munich, a distance of 2,615 nautical miles, in 6hr 15min and landed with 2,350kg of fuel remaining, enough for a further 150 nautical miles flying, plus 30min holding.

Herr Schörgruber had become the major shareholder in Bavaria Flug in 1974 and was now the owner of Bavaria Germanair, but sold his interest to Hapag-Lloyd in April 1977. As a result it was decided to merge Bavaria Germanair with Hapag-Lloyd Fluggesellschaft mbH, a subsidiary of the Hapag-Lloyd AG shipping group, but a full merger of the two airlines was not approved by West Germany's Federal Cartel Office until January 1979. D-AMAS and D-AMAT appeared with Hapg-Lloyd titles a few months later, as did several of the other One-Elevens. As part of the merger conditions Herr Schörgruber retained the right to use the name Bavaria and proposed to start a new airline with three One-Eleven 500s acquired from Hapag-Lloyd, but in the end nothing came of this.

Hapag-Lloyd had started charter and IT operations from Bremen in the spring of 1973 with three Boeing 727-100s, six more being acquired

later, as well as an A300C4-200 Airbus. Germanair had likewise taken delivery of its first A300B-4 Airbus on 23 May 1975, three more Airbuses later joined the Bavaria Germanair fleet. The build-up of Airbus capacity enabled the One-Eleven 528s D-ALFA and D-ANUE to be sold to British Caledonian on 30 October 1981 as G-BJRT and G-BJRU, while three more One-Elevens were sold to Austral of Argentina. D-AMOR became LV-PFR and then LV-OAX, and D-AMUC became LV-OAY, these two being delivered from Frankfurt in December 1979 and the end of January 1980, while D-AMAS became LV-PEW and then LV-OAZ at about the same time. D-AMAM was sold to Dan-Air Services in 1981 as G-AZPZ, and D-AMAT was sold to Air Malawi as 7Q-YKK.

Austral of Argentina, like Bavaria, had been a successful operator of the One-Eleven 400, and followed this with a firm order for three Series 521s. These, registered LV-JNR, LV-JNS and LV-JNT, were all delivered in November 1969 and went into service on the routes from Buenos Aires down to Patagonia and to towns in the northern and northeastern parts of the country. LV-JNR was leased to Sadia SA Transportes Aereos of Brazil in September 1970 as PP-SDP pending delivery of their first One-Eleven 520, and in April 1971 it was sold to Court Line Aviation Ltd as G-AYXB. As traffic built up in the mid and late 1970s, Austral took the opportunity to add to its fleet by acquiring some One-Eleven 500s being sold off by European operators. In addition to the three ex-Bavaria Germanair ones mentioned previously, there was the ex-British Caledonian Series 509, G-AWWY, which was first leased and then sold to Austral, finally becoming LV-LHT.

The One-Eleven 529 HB-ITL (ex-G-16-13) delivered to the Swiss charter operator Phoenix Airways of Basle on 1 April 1971 was also acquired and became LV-LOX. Phoenix had been formed in October 1970 to operate ad hoc charters and inclusive tour flights from Basle, and also operated a leased Boeing 707 for a time. Sadly LV-LOX crashed into the River Plate on 7 May 1981 while landing at the Buenos Aires Aeroparque airport en route from Tucuman, with the loss of all 30 people on board. The crash occurred during one of the

Top right:
D-AMOR was one of four 114-passenger One-Eleven 524s ordered by the German charter operator Germanair of Frankfurt for inclusive tour flights to Mediterranean and North African holiday resorts.

Right:
Bavaria merged with Germanair on 1 January 1977, and One-Eleven 528 D-ALFA *Jakob Fugger* is seen here in the new Bavaria Germanair livery, being refuelled for a return flight to Germany.

Inset above:
Austral's third One-Eleven 521 LV-JNT wearing BAC's Class B registration G-16-10 and the letters of Austral's partner airline ALA before the two merged in June 1971; LV-JNT was delivered in November 1969.

Above:
The first production One-Eleven 510 for BEA, G-AVMH, shows the brisk take-off of which the new stretched version was capable. Engines of BEA's fleet were 12,000lb st Spey 512-14s without water injection.

Below:
G-AXMH *Halcyon Sun*. Court Line was one of the largest
British operators of the One-Eleven.

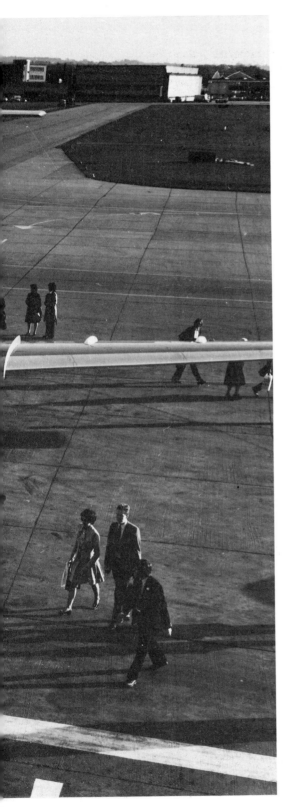

worst storms ever recorded over Buenos Aires. Austral also acquired the ex-Court Line Series 518 TG-AVA from Aviateca of Guatemala, this becoming LV-MRZ, and from Sadia another ex-Court Line Series 518, PT-TYX, which became LV-MEX on 28 January 1978. Another Austral One-Eleven 500 is LV-MZM. In 1979 the airline supplemented its One-Elevens with a pair of DC-9 Series 51s leased from the makers pending delivery of five DC-9 Super 80s ordered.

The only other South American customer for the One-Eleven 500 was the Brazilian airline Sadia SA Transportes Aereos of Sao Paulo, which ordered two Series 520s early in 1969 and a third later. Pending delivery of the first, PP-SDQ, on 15 October 1970, Series 521 LV-JNR was leased from Austral in September as PP-SDP; the second, PP-SDR, was delivered on 31 December and the third, PP-SDS, followed on 23 September 1972. They went into service on Sadia's extensive domestic network in the eastern part of Brazil, mainly from Sao Paulo and Porto Alegre, and extending as far north as Belem and down the Amazon to Manaus; the One-Elevens supplemented Handley Page Herald turboprops, of which seven were eventually ordered. Sadia's plans for the One-Eleven included the use of an 86-passenger mixed-class interior to reduce its present fare levels; later, a 109-passenger interior was featured.

In June 1972 Sadia changed its name to Transbrasil SA Linhas Aereas, and during 1973-74 three One-Eleven 523s were acquired from British Midland Airways, while the latter also bought three of Transbrasil's Heralds in March 1973. The three BMA One-Elevens, G-AXLL, G-AXLM and G-AXLN, became respectively PP-SDT, PP-SDV and PP-SDU, the first of these being delivered in March 1973. Two more ex-Court Line Series 518s were leased late in 1974, G-AXMF becoming PT-TYX and G-AXML was PT-TYW. The first of these was delivered on 6 December, and was returned to the UK in November 1977, later becoming LV-MEX with Austral, while PT-TYW became TG-AVA with Aviateca of Guatemala in September 1975; Aviateca also acquired the ex-British Midland PP-SDU as TG-AYA after its return to BAC. Transbrasil had also leased Series 530 G-AZMF from B.Cal as PT-TYY from February to December 1974. That year Transbrasil had taken delivery of the first of two Boeing 727-100s and as more 727s were acquired the remaining One-Elevens were disposed of, PP-SDR and PP-SDV being returned to

Left:
Passengers disembarking from One-Eleven 529 HB-ITL of the Basle-based charter operator Phoenix Airways. This was later sold to Austral as LV-LOX.

BAC, PP-SDT being sold to Faucett of Peru as OB-R-1137, and PP-SDS being sold to Tiger Air as N110TA.

The three British Midland One-Eleven 523s had been ordered in 1969, two on 3 June and the third on 16 July that year, and the first, G-AXLL, was delivered on 17 February 1970 and the two others in March. They were used for extensive inclusive tour charter operations to European holiday centres from East Midlands Airport at Castle Donington, Leicestershire, but after British Midland decided to relinquish group charter and IT flights in favour of concentrating on scheduled services the One-Elevens were sold. At first Viscount 810s and Heralds were used for these scheduled routes, but in 1976 British Midland introduced the first of several DC-9s when it put a DC-9 Series 10 into service on the heavier-trafficked routes; it now has six DC-9 Series 15s and two DC-9 Series 32s. Prior to their sale to Transbrasil One-Elevens G-AXLM and G-AXLN were both leased to Court Line Aviation for a time. The first of these, together with another ex-Transbrasil Series 520, were later acquired by Arkia Israel Inland Airlines Ltd, in which El Al has a 50% financial holding, to operate domestic routes in Israel and charters. Series 520 PP-SDR became G-BEKA and then G-16-22 after it was returned to the UK, and in July 1977 it was acquired by Arkia as 4X-BAR, soon becoming 4X-AHS; it was delivered on 16 August from Hurn via Athens, and after some months in Arkia service was restored as G-BEKA in 1978, being sold to

Dan-Air the following year. The ex-British Midland Series 523 PP-SDV had been returned to BAC on 11 December 1976, becoming G-AXLM again and later G-16-23, and this was delivered to Arkia on 20 May 1978 as 4X-BAR (previously 4X-BAS) after having been leased by BAC to Cyprus Airways for several months in 1977. After serving with Arkia it was sold to Philippine Air Lines as RP-C1193, being delivered from Hurn on 7 July 1980.

In Central America and the Caribbean the One-Eleven 500 also made its mark, building on the successful operations of the Series 400 in that area. Aviateca – Empresa Guatemalteca de Aviacion SA – was the first Central American customer for the One-Eleven 500, the airline's president, Colonel Aguilar, issuing a statement in Guatemala City in November 1970 that the British aircraft had been chosen after examination of 16 competing submissions from other manufacturers; the airline would probably purchase one to start with, and take options on more. One-Eleven operations in fact started about a week after Aviateca's president revealed his choice, when Series 518 G-AXMK leased from Court Line as TG-ARA entered service on the more important international routes from Guatemala City to Miami, New Orleans and several Central American cities. Aviateca's own 99-passenger One-Eleven 516 TG-AZA *Quetzal* was delivered on 25 March 1971 in a pleasing yellow and orange livery; this had originally been destined for Philippine Air Lines as PI-C1191 and it replaced TG-ARA, which was returned from lease and

restored as G-AXMK on 6 April 1971. Another ex-Court Line Series 518 PT-TYW was acquired from Transbrasil and became TG-AVA in September 1975; while still with Court Line as G-AXML this had also been leased to LANICA of Nicaragua as AN-BHJ from December 1971 to 28 March 1972, when it was restored to the UK register; it was later sold to Austral as LV-MRZ. Another ex-Transbrasil and British Midland Series 523, PP-SDU (ex-G-AXLN), was acquired through BAC as TG-AYA, this being delivered in April 1978. In late May that year it was acquired by Cayman Airways as VR-CAL *Cayman Victory*. The Series 516 TG-AZA *Quetzal* was sold to Philippine Air Lines in 1980 as RP-C1194.

Bahamas Airways and LACSA of Costa Rica were two other Caribbean operators of the One-Eleven 500 which had previously used the Series 400. An order for two One-Eleven 517s for Bahamas Airways with one on option was announced in September 1968, the one on option was taken up in June 1970, and a fourth was to have been delivered that November. The first two, VP-BCN and VP-BCO, were delivered on 23 and 29 July 1969 and seated 99 passengers, but the third, VP-BCQ, was not in fact taken up, and the fourth (which would have been VP-BCR) was not delivered because the airline went into liquidation on 9 October 1970. The Series 517s entered service on the Nassau-Freeport-Miami 'Golden Triangle' routes and between Nassau and Freeport, this being the only Bahamian domestic route operated by jets. Big traffic

increases had resulted on all these One-Eleven routes, and the two Series 517s also operated 'casino specials' – flights specially for American gamblers playing the roulette tables in the Bahamas casinos; a One-Eleven left Miami at 9pm each night for the 35min 'casino special' flight to Freeport, returning at 2am the following morning. But the One-Eleven's undoubted success in Bahamas Airways service was not sufficient to prevent the airline's financial demise, and the two Series 517s were flown back to the UK after the collapse and went into storage for a time at Wisley.

After Court Line acquired a 75% interest in Leeward Island Air Transport Services Ltd – LIAT – in November 1971 for £1.6million as part of its Caribbean expansion plans, which involved heavy investment in hotels in the region and developing holiday bookings from the USA, it leased Series 518 G-AXMK to LIAT as VP-LAK on purchasing the airline. It then acquired the third Bahamas Airways Series 517, which was to have been VP-BCQ but was not delivered, for immediate lease to LIAT and this was delivered to LIAT's Antigua base in June 1972 as VP-LAN; it featured a 350gal auxiliary fuel tank in the freight hold and had a 100-passenger all economy class interior with provision for a hot meal service in flight. Painted in LIAT's new mauve colour scheme, VP-LAN replaced VP-LAK which returned to the UK and was restored on 5 July 1972 as G-AXMK, and the new One-Eleven was intended to spearhead the development of LIAT's routes further afield. The first two Series 517s of Bahamas

Airways were also bought by Court Line for use by LIAT, VP-BCN and VP-BCO becoming G-AZEB and G-AZEC respectively, the former being delivered on 8 December 1971, and entering service with LIAT as VP-LAP in November 1972, while G-AZEC became VP-LAR the following month.

LIAT had been formed in 1956 and started services with a Piper Apache between Antigua and Montserrat; the airline soon became a subsidiary of British West Indian Airways and developed inter-island services in the Virgin Islands, to Puerto Rico and Guadeloupe. Routes were extended southwards through the Leeward and Windward Islands to Trinidad and Tobago, and also to Kingston in Jamaica. The One-Elevens supplemented the six HS.748 Series 2 turboprops already in service, while five Islanders were used on the shorter inter-island routes. Shortly before the Court Line collapse in 1974 LIAT suffered from fuel price rises, inflation and a slump in American overseas travel, and the One-Elevens returned to the UK, VP-LAP being delivered to Hurn on 7 March 1974 becoming G-AZEB again, and VP-LAR being restored as G-AZEC on 1 April 1974, while VP-LAN became G-BCCV in May. These three, together with the Court Line Series 518s G-AXMH, G-AXMI and G-AXMJ, were all ferried to Hurn for BAC on 11 September. The first two were later sold to Philippine Air Lines, G-AZEB becoming RP-C1186 and leaving on delivery on 27 September 1975, while G-AZEC became RP-C1187 in November 1975.

The former VP-LAN, now G-BCCV, was leased long-term to Monarch Airlines as G-BCXR, and was delivered at Luton on 7 March 1975. Monarch also acquired two more Court Line One-Eleven 518s on lease through BAC: G-AXMG after its return on 24 November 1975 from going on an earlier lease to Cyprus Airways in May 1974 as 5B-DAF; and G-AXMJ, which was delivered on a long-term lease on 28 February 1975 as G-BCWG – this was leased again by BAC to Cyprus Airways in 1976. Monarch's One-Elevens supplemented the airline's Boeing 720Bs, now superseded by 737-200s and 757s in operating charter and IT flights from the UK to holiday resorts in Europe and on the Mediterranean, and also from Berlin. Monarch had also acquired One-Eleven 509 G-AWWZ *Isle of Eriskay* from B.Cal on 14 November 1975.

Court Line (Aviation) Ltd had changed its name from Autair International Airways Ltd with effect from 1 January 1970 to coincide with the delivery of the first of five One-Eleven 518s, G-AXMF *Halcyon Breeze*, on 5 December 1969. Two of the three options placed with the original order were 'firmed up' in the spring of 1969, and a further two ordered in the summer of 1971 so that, together with the three acquired for LIAT and one Series 521 LV-JNR acquired from Austral as G-AYXB *Halcyon Bay*, Court Line was one of the largest One-Eleven 500 operators apart from BEA. In the belief that holiday flights should be fun, and that an informal holiday atmosphere should be created for the passenger right at the start, a new holiday image was introduced at Court Line as the first One-Eleven 518s were delivered, in which aircraft, vehicles, tickets and even stationery were identified by bold shades of green, turquoise or pink. The new One-Elevens were painted in pastel shades of pink, turquoise or orange, and the stewardesses wore bright informal pinafore dresses in colours to match the aircraft's exterior; the interior cabin decors also featured these bright colours. The new colour schemes were the work of Mr Peter Murdoch and his wife, who were also the graphic designers for the 1968 Mexico Olympics. The 'Halcyon' motif was stressed in aircraft names, such as *Halcyon Sky* (G-AXMG) and *Halcyon Sun* (G-AXMJ), and although the practice was quite common in the States it was still a rare thing for a British airline to embark on a corporate restyling of this extent. The One-Elevens seated 109 passengers and had provision for full blind landing facilities.

The new jets, like the earlier Series 400s, were used solely on inclusive tour flights, in particular for Clarksons Holidays, which offered mass travel at the bottom end of the holiday market. But this was just the area that was first to feel the impact of the fuel price rises following the 1973 Arab-Israeli war, and the first chill wind of the oncoming world recession, although when Clarkson Holidays was in danger of bankruptcy in April 1973, Court Line had stepped in and rescued it. Another of the airline's major tour operator customers, the rather more up-market Horizon Holidays, was likewise taken over for a nominal £1 at the beginning of 1974 after it was in danger of folding up. The 1973 summer season had seen the introduction of the first two Lockheed TriStars in Europe, seating 400 passengers each, by Court Line; each of these could do the work of four One-Elevens but equally, if one was delayed with 400 passengers aboard it gained far more adverse publicity than four separate delays of aircraft with 100 passengers. But the TriStars were too big and inflexible for what

Right:
One-Eleven RP-C1194 was originally to have been PI-C1191 of Philippine Air Lines but instead was delivered to Aviateca of Guatemala in March 1971 as TG-AZA *Quetzal*, being sold to PAL in 1980 as RP-C1194.

Below right:
LACSA of Costa Rica acquired three One-Eleven 531s to follow its Series 409s; TI-1084C seen here was the first, entering service in June 1971. It later became TI-LRF and then TI-LRL *Arenal*, and was leased to Cayman Airways Ltd as VR-CAB *Cayman Progress*.
D. Spurgeon via J. M. G. Gradidge

was becoming a recession-hit holiday market and they exacerbated the airline's financial difficulties. In June 1974 the Court Line Group's shipbuilding and ship repair interests were sold to the British Government for £16million in the hope of saving the holiday and airline sides of the Group, at least until the end of the 1974 holiday season. But this did not prove to be possible, and Court Line announced on 15 August that year that it was going into liquidation, which it did leaving some 49,000 tourists stranded overseas, who were flown home by other airlines. Court had tried and failed to expand its way out of its financial difficulties.

Apart from the ex-Court One-Eleven 518s leased to Transbrasil and Monarch Airlines, as related earlier, four of them went to Dan-Air Services Ltd on long-term lease from January and February 1975, G-AXMH and G-AXMI being re-registered G-BDAS and G-BDAE; G-AXMK went to Dan-Air as G-BCWA, and G-AYOR became G-BDAT, while G-AYOP *Halcyon Beach* had been sold to B.Cal early in 1973. Dan-Air also acquired Series 509s G-AWWX and G-AXYD from British Caledonian and the Series 515 D-AMAM, which became G-AZPZ, from Bavaria Germanair in 1981, this later going to B.Cal on long-term lease on 1 March 1982, and being named *City of Glasgow*. Dan-Air also acquired the ex-Arkia Series 520 G-BEKA (ex-4X-AHS) in 1979, and three Series 515s from LACSA of Costa Rica, G-BJYL, G-BJYM and G-BJMV. Dan-Air built up its fleet of 11 One-Eleven 500s from acquiring used aircraft, rather than ordering from the makers, and the BAC jets are used on European inclusive tour flights from UK cities and also scheduled services. Dan-Air also leased Series 525 YR-BCQ from TAROM as G-TARO for six months from 28 March 1984, and the lease was later extended to the end of summer 1985.

Philippine Air Lines Inc, which had operated Series 402s successfully, ordered four One-Eleven 527s in mid-1970, plus two more late in 1973. The first four were PI-C1161, PI-C1171, PI-C1181 and PI-C1191, of which the first was delivered on 26 October 1971, although it had first flown as G-AYOS a year earlier, on 30 September 1970; it was written off in an accident on 23 May 1976. The second, PI-C1171, was temporarily registered G-AYKN to BAC for a demonstration in Rumania on 20-22 October 1970, and PI-C1191 was not delivered but went instead to Aviateca as TG-AZA *Quetzal*, being eventually sold back to PAL in 1980 as RP-C1194. The next two, RP-C1182 and RP-C1183, were delivered on 8 June and 5 July 1974 registered with the new RP-C nationality prefix introduced in 1973, which was also applied to the first three One-Eleven 527s. RP-C1183 was christened *Imelda* after the President's wife, Mrs Imelda Marcos, and was used as a Presidential and government VIP transport.

The BAC jets were generating a continually growing traffic volume in PAL service and this, together with the taking over by PAL on 2 January 1974 of two other domestic airlines, Air Manila and Filipinas Orient Airways, with their routes and staff, created a demand for more One-Eleven capacity, as PAL was now nominated by the Government as the sole national operator of both domestic and overseas routes. As related earlier, two more One-Elevens, RP-C1184 and RP-C1185, were acquired from Bavaria Germanair in 1974, two ex-LIAT and Court Line ones, RP-C1186 and RP-C1187, in 1975, one Series 501 RP-C1188 (ex-G-AXJL) from B.Cal in 1977, followed by the ex-Monarch and Court Line RP-C1189 (ex-G-BCWG), one ex-Arkia Series 523 RP-C1193 (ex-4X-BAR) and the ex-Aviateca RP-C1194.

This build-up of One-Eleven capacity made possible major increases in frequency on the domestic trunk routes, and also the release of DC-8s from the Manila-Zamboanga and Manila-Cebu routes as a fuel conservation measure and their replacement by the BAC jets. It also coincided with President Marcos' plan to develop more airfields in the Philippines serving the remote centres of population to take the One-Elevens and spread wider the benefits of jet service. The BAC jet was the most profitable aircraft in PAL's entire fleet, with tremendous passenger appeal and exceptional reliability; in PAL service it carried up to 104 passengers.

One-Eleven RP-C1184 has what must be the unique distinction of suffering not one but two separate bomb explosions in flight and surviving both these attempts at sabotage. The first occurred near Manila on 6 June 1975 when a bomb went off in the rear toilet, but luckily there were no fatalities among the 58 passengers and five crew and the One-Eleven was landed safely. After temporary patching up it was flown back to BAC at Hurn on 9 August for permanent repairs, returning to Manila on 22 February 1976. The second in-flight explosion occurred on 18 August 1978 and this time one person on board was killed and three were injured; again the bomb had been placed in the rear toilet and the damage to the port fuselage was similar to that caused by the earlier bomb. The One-Eleven was flown back to Britain without pressurisation and below 12,000ft for repairs at Hurn, and it returned on 27 March 1979 after a rebuild and fitting of a 'wide body'-look cabin interior. One-Eleven RP-C1182 was badly damaged in a forced landing at Manila on 17 February 1981, and in August 1984 it overran the runway on landing at Tacloban and ended up in the sea.

LACSA of Costa Rica, like PAL, operated both the Series 400 and 500, and ordered one One-Eleven 531 at the end of 1971 and two more the following summer, plus a fourth later on. The first Series 531, TI-1084C, formerly G-AYWB, was leased from BAC and later bought outright; it entered service in June 1971 and was deployed on the San Jose-Miami-Mexico City triangle of high density routes, and it enabled LACSA to extend jet services beyond Panama on to recently awarded routes to Barranquilla in Colombia and Maracaibo and Caracas in Venezuela. The second, TI-1095C, was delivered on 6 November 1972 and the third, TI-1096C, on 14 May 1973; following the introduction of all-letter registrations on the first day of 1975 TI-1084C, the first, became TI-LRF and later TI-LRL Arenal, while TI-1095C became TI-LRI Poas, and TI-1096C became TI-LRJ Barracuda, later Chirripo. TI-LRL was leased to Cayman Airways Ltd, the national airline of the Cayman Islands, as VR-CAB Cayman Progress, and linked Georgetown on Grand Cayman to Kingston (Jamaica) and Miami, and more recently to Houston (Texas). Cayman Airways also acquired Series 523 VR-CAL Cayman Victory from Aviateca, with which it had been TG-AYA, in May 1978; it was withdrawn from

use at Miami in December 1982. It was sold early in 1984 to British Island Airways along with VR-CAB, these two being restored as G-AXLN and G-AYWB respectively, and they are now named Island Enterprise and Island Envoy. TI-LRJ had also been leased to Cayman Airways before VR-CAL, since about 1974. LACSA's fourth One-Eleven was TI-LRK, the ex-Paninternational D-ALAS and G-AZPE, delivered in December 1973 and named first Paso and later Arenal. In 1981 TI-LRI, TI-LRJ and TI-LRK were sold to Dan-Air Services as G-BJYM, G-BJMV and G-BJYL respectively, although TI-LRI was first leased to TACA of El Salvador for a time early in 1982.

TAROMS's order for five One-Eleven 525s, placed through Technoimportexport in the spring of 1975, and the associated Rumanian production arrangements, are discussed in the previous chapter. These five are YR-BCI to YR-BCM (the first of which was delivered on 21 March 1977 and the last on 25 August that year) and they seat up to 104 passengers. Last airline customer for the One-Eleven 500 was Cyprus Airways, which ordered two Series 537s in the summer of 1976 and had first used the type when it leased Series 518 G-AXMG from Court Line as 5B-DAF in May 1974, this being returned as G-AXMG in November 1975. This was followed by the ex-Monarch Series 518 G-BCWG leased from the makers from 1976 until February 1978, and then by the ex-Transbrasil Series 523 G-AXLM leased in 1977 which went to Arkia at the beginning of 1978. Of the two Series 537s, 5B-DAG was delivered on 8 December 1977 and 5B-DAH on 28 January 1978, and they were followed by a third, 5B-DAJ, that arrived on 6 October 1978. 5B-DAH was damaged on the ground in a gun battle at Larnaca Airport during a DC-8 hi-jacking attempt, and was flown back to Hurn for repairs on 22 February 1978, leaving for Cyprus after repairs on 19 April. 5B-DAJ was leased to British Airways from 15 October 1978 to 28 April 1980 as G-BFWN.

Below:
One-Eleven 537 5B-DAG was the first of three for Cyprus Airways, being delivered on 5 December 1977. These are used chiefly for regional services from Larnaca Airport to the Middle East.

Further One-Eleven Developements

Meanwhile, with the One-Eleven 500 and 475 successfully flight tested and in airline service, work continued on future developments for the middle and late 1970s. Current in 1968 were design studies of the One-Eleven 600 seating up to 130 passengers and powered by an uprated aft-fan version of the Rolls-Royce Spey giving 17,000lb-18,000lb st. Later the designation Series 600 was given to the One-Eleven variant offered to British Airways in competition with the Boeing 737-200, of which the state airline announced its decision to order 19 in April 1978. The Series 600 as submitted to BA was basically a Series 500 with the revised wing of the Series 670 and engine silencers, and British Aerospace also proposed that the Series 600 could later be re-engined with the new Rolls-Royce RB.432 turbofans in the 16,000-18,000lb thrust class under the designation One-Eleven 700. British Airways told BAe that it would be prepared to buy this RB.432-powered version if it was available but could not wait until 1985, although it found the Series 700 promising. In the end BA chose the 737 at a cost of £140million for the 19 ordered, thus effectively depriving any future One-Eleven developments of most of the necessary home market they would have needed as a launching base.

BAe put out a statement when British Airways 737-200 plans became known in which it stressed the One-Eleven's merits, pointing out that the same number could have been ordered at a total cost of £129million, and that their purchase would save about $250million in foreign exchange, provide additional employment in the UK and help BAe's efforts in the all-important export markets. The statement also pointed out that the British Airways assumption, based on detailed traffic forecasts up to 1994, that the larger 737 could generate a greater operating surplus over 14 years, was open to a wide potential margin of error since a 1% difference in operating costs through unforeseen commercial or political factors would make a difference of £15million in the comparative figures. But in spite of these arguments, with both the Department of Trade and BAe being shown the state airline's figures justifying the order, Government approval for the 737 order was given in July 1978.

Studies of several 120-130-passenger develop-ments for the 1980s continued for a time under the Series 700 designation, but this originally applied to the projected stretched and quieter version announced in mid-1974, with a 12ft longer fuselage than the Series 500 seating 119-134 passengers in a 'wide-body' look cabin. Powerplant would have been the proposed 16,900lb st Spey 67C (or Spey 606) with a new front fan and a higher by-pass ratio than current Speys for improved fuel economy, giving a range of up to 2,300 miles. The Spey 67C featured a three-stage low pressure compressor driven by a three-stage low pressure turbine instead of the five-stage low pressure compressor and two-stage turbine of the Spey 512-14. The increased air mass flow and by-pass ratio reduced jet noise, as well as giving a 6% better cruise specific fuel consumption. Noise was further reduced by pre-mixing the hot and cold gas streams before the final nozzle, deleting the inlet guide vanes and by various other changes, while quietness was also improved by acoustic linings in the by-pass duct and jet pipe. Maximum gross weight of the Series 700 would have been 117,000lb, and BAC did have some talks with prospective airline customers for this particular variant.

Developed in parallel with the Series 700 was the Series 800 of 1975, an altogether more ambitious derivative. It would have been powered by two SNECMA/GEC CFM56 turbofans of 22,000lb st, and would have had accommodation for 144-161 passengers in a fuselage stretched by no less than 32ft 6in over the Series 500's, with a 24ft 2in fuselage 'plug' added forward of the wings and an 8ft 4in section added behind them, a 'wide-body' look cabin being featured. The span would have been increased by 10ft over the Series 500's, and there would have been a new centre-section. Maximum take-off weight was 137,000lb and the maximum range 2,400 miles. The CFM56 turbofan had a by-pass ratio of 6.0:1, and it was claimed to be quiet enough to keep community noise 'footprints' entirely within the airport boundaries. The Series 800 was proposed to Air France as a Caravelle replacement and, had it been built, would have competed directly with the Boeing 737-300 and DC-9 Super 80, while the Series 700 would have contended with the DC-9 Series 50 in the battle for orders.

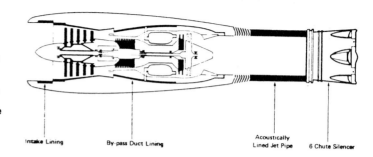

Intake Lining   By-pass Duct Lining   Acoustically Lined Jet Pipe   6 Chute Silencer

Both the Series 700 and 800 were succeeded in 1976 by the proposed X-Eleven, a bigger, quieter and more fuel-efficient development of the Series 800 with accommodation for 130-160 passengers six-abreast in a wider-bodied cabin of 11ft 11in width, with the 'wide-body' cabin look. This should have overcome the competitive advantage that the Boeing 737 had over both the One-Eleven and DC-9 in having six-abreast seating instead of their five-abreast, which had stemmed from the use of the 707's basic upper fuselage cross-section and much of the 707 jigs and tooling for the short-haul 737, as well as the 727. The X-Eleven would have been powered by two of the new high by-pass ratio turbofans of 10 tonnes (22,000lb-24,500lb) thrust such as the CFM56 or Pratt & Whitney JT10D. The X-Eleven would have retained about 40% commonality with the One-Eleven 500, having the same nose and rear fuselage sections, the same wings, fin and tailplane with appropriate root-section extensions for a greater wing span, allied to the new wider fuselage; a strengthened undercarriage for the higher design weights would have been featured. Maximum take-off weight would have been 140,000lb and the X-Eleven could have operated from runways of 5,000-7,000ft; its full load range would have been about 2,300 miles. Work on the X-Eleven had reached a fairly advanced stage of design before it was decided by British Aerospace to discontinue it in favour of the proposed European collaborative programme for a 160-seat airliner known as Jet, from the initials of the Joint Engineering Team set up in September 1977 by Aerospatiale, BAe, Fokker-VFW and Messerschmitt-Bolkow-Blohm, to study such a project. But this too failed to emerge as anything definite.

While design work was proceeding on the various stretched and more powerful One-Eleven developments, work had also been going ahead on a number of product improvements that could be fitted to existing One-Eleven variants either on the production line or retrospectively. The forward freight door and associated cargo handling system, the 'wide-body' cabin look conversion, Category 2 autoland, an inertial navigation system and gravel runway protection (standard on the Series 475 but also available as a kit) have all been described earlier while the various auxiliary fuel systems available for extended range, and used chiefly in executive One-Elevens, could also be fitted for airline use, such as delivery flights or for longer range on inclusive tour flights. A nylon/cotton freight container that could be used for light freight, mail and express parcels and could be secured to the passenger seats was made available for airline use; this converted a triple passenger seat unit into a 500lb freight unit. An enclosed overhead hatrack and hand baggage rack was another improvement that could be retrofitted to existing One-Elevens.

Probably the most important of all the various product improvements offered for the One-Eleven was the engine 'hush kit' developed jointly by BAC and Rolls-Royce to bring the type's community noise levels within the ICAO Annex 16 and American FAR Part 36 requirements, which promulgated new noise regulations. This kit was designed to reduce the area within the 90 EPNdB (Equivalent Perceived Noise Decibels) noise contour by approximately 50%, giving a noise 'footprint' equivalent to that of one of the older twin turboprops or the current big trijet airliners. The hush kit consists of an intake duct lining, a by-pass duct lining, an extended acoustically lined jet pipe and a six-chute jet mixing exhaust silencer; a hush kit was first flown on the prototype One-Eleven 475 G-ASYD on 14 June 1974. Production hush kits became available for retrofitting from late 1975, and the first new production aircraft to be fitted with them was the first One-Eleven 525 for TAROM, YR-BCI, which made its first flight on 20 December 1976. These kits did impose certain performance penalties, but these proved to be lower than estimated, with a thrust loss of 0.75% on take-off instead of the estimated 1%, and a 2% increase in fuel consumption instead of the 3.3% forecast.

There was a slight increase in weight, although the installed weight of production hush kits is less than 400lb.

For the Series 670 a further hush kit refinement was a newly-developed acoustically-lined ejector silencer which was flown on the prototype, G-ASYD, in the spring of 1979. This consists basically of a retractable acoustically-lined sleeve which is extended for take-off and landing to mask the high frequency noise tones generated by the six-chute exhaust silencer. This new silencer will, according to BAe, reduce the 100 EPNdB noise 'footprint' by 75% and weight penalty is less than that of the standard hush kit.

The Tay One-Eleven

Various refanned and uprated versions of the Rolls-Royce Spey had been considered for developments of the One-Eleven over some 15 years before an agreement announced in March 1983 between Rolls and Gulfstream Aerospace (formerly Grumman American Aviation) on a large order for the new, quieter and more fuel efficient RB.183-03 Tay to power the Gulfstream IV executive jet made it possible to propose this engine for the One-Eleven, both for new aircraft and for retrofitting to existing ones. Rated at 13,500lb st at sea level, the Tay is a straightforward development of the Spey 555 with a new front fan of 44in diameter to increase the by-pass ratio from less than 1:1 to 3:1; it has an advanced low pressure turbine and a high pressure system with a low emission combustion chamber being developed from the core of the latest RB.183 Spey 555. It also incorporates other high efficiency components developed in the Rolls-Royce advanced engineering and RB.211 programmes, and embodies the latest experience with high efficiency wide-chord fan blades.

The first Tay turbofan made its first test bed runs in August 1984, and the first Tay-powered One-Eleven is planned to make its maiden flight in May 1986, with certification in the autumn of that year, and deliveries of production Tays for retrofit installations starting shortly thereafter; such an installation could be carried out without necessitating any changes in the current design weights. The name Tay, incidentally, was first applied to a slightly larger and more powerful development of the well-known centrifugal-flow Rolls-Royce Nene, the second prototype Viscount first flying with two 6,250lb st, RTa.1 Tays in underslung nacelles not unlike the Boeing 737's on 15 March 1950. The Tay did not go into production in this country, but was built in large numbers under licence by Pratt & Whitney as the J48 for the Grumman F9F Panther and Cougar, while in France Hispano-Suiza built a developed version of the Tay known as the Verdon to power the Dassault Mystère IV.

A number of One-Eleven operators have noted that the aircraft's excellent long-life structure would make re-engining with Tays very worthwhile, especially from the viewpoint of compliance with all foreseeable international noise regulations, such as those contained in Chapters 2 and 3 of ICAO Annex 16 and the American FAR Part 36 Stage 3 rules. An important consideration to all UK-based operators is that with Tays fitted the One-Eleven could easily meet the London Airports 'Night Operational' Noise Contour Area Limit requirements, which existing One-Elevens, even with hush kits, cannot, when taking off. Meeting these night noise requirements will permit compliance with rules for night operation at many other airports, with corresponding advantages in more versatile route scheduling and higher utilisation; also, the payment of excess landing charges ('Noise Tax') levied at many airports would be avoided.

With Tays fitted, fuel consumption would be reduced by up to 15%, and this would give a significant improvement in range that would typically allow non-stop operation from the UK to existing holiday resort destinations in North Africa,

the Greek Islands, or Tenerife in the Canary Islands. Maximum range increases of about 25% (between 300 and 400 nautical miles) will be possible from a given airfield, and the Tays will also give an all-round improvement in operational performance, notably in take-off distances. For the executive One-Eleven 400 operators, where installation of auxiliary fuel tankage currently gives a marginal transatlantic capability, a re-engining with Tays will give them up to 690 miles more range, resulting in a maximum range of up to 4,200 miles with NBAA (National Business Aircraft Association of the USA) VFR (Visual Flight Rules) reserves and a typical executive payload of 1,500lb. Another advantage for both executive and airline use is that the costly demineralised water used in the Spey's water injection system will not be necesary in the higher-powered Tay.

The same Tay nacelle or pod as fitted to the new Gulfstream IV will be used for the One-Eleven with a minimum of modification, some changes being made to the engine stub structure, and there will be some strengthening of the existing fuselage engine frames to cater for the Tay's greater angle of offset and increased weight. Target-type thrust reversers will replace the present cascade type, and removing the water injection system will result in a weight saving of about 300lb plus 1,000lb of water.

The One-Eleven has shown itself outstandingly well able to withstand the hard pounding of intensive short-haul operations, and several

Below:
The original One-Eleven 700 project of mid-1974 would have had a 12ft longer fuselage than the Series 500, seating from 119 to 134 passengers in a 'wide-body' look cabin. Powerplant would have been the refanned Spey 67C (or Spey 606) of 16,900lb st with reduced jet noise and lower fuel consumption.

One-Eleven 203s and 204s of US Air (formerly Allegheny Airlines) have now logged more than 60,000 landings, while several British Airways Series 510s have achieved more than 30,000 landings. The One-Eleven 200, 400 and 500 airframes have all now been cleared by a Structural Integrity Audit to a life of 85,000 flight cycles from take-off to landing, which should be amply sufficient to justify a decision to re-engine with Tays.

But the question must remain – why was more not done to develop the One-Eleven beyond the Series 500 and 475? By 1970, with over 200 sold, the One-Eleven was the largest earner of foreign exchange among British civil aircraft then being exported, and Britain's biggest ever single dollar earner, even against a 10% US tariff barrier. BAC's basic launching investment of around £30 million in the overall One-Eleven programme had been complemented by partnership launching aid of £18.75million from the Government that was repaid by a substantial levy on each aircraft sold. By 1970 One-Eleven production costs had for some time been sufficiently below competitive market prices to achieve a healthy profit margin on each aircraft built, and this made a significant contribution to paying off launching and development costs, so that the programme was certainly economically viable as a basis for future developments.

The year 1965, when the One-Eleven had entered airline service, had been a grim one for the aircraft industry with the cancellation of the BAC TSR.2, the Hawker P.1154 and HS.681. The industry was in the political doghouse, and the Plowden Committee reflected the fashionably defeatist views then current about its prospects; these were views that for some years heavily coloured any proposals for further investment in new aircraft or engine

TAY-POWERED BAC ONE-ELEVEN 500
GENERAL ARRANGEMENT

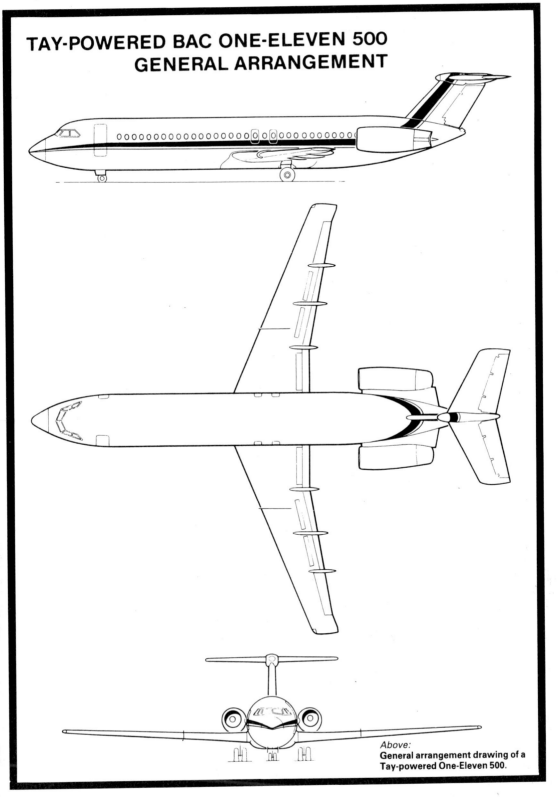

Above:
**General arrangement drawing of a
Tay-powered One-Eleven 500.**

projects. But in spite of this the One-Eleven order book grew, and BAC was sufficiently confident by 1967 to unveil the Two-Eleven project, a 203-passenger airliner resembling a scaled-up One-Eleven and aimed at BEA's needs, with two early RB.211-06 turbofans of 34,900lb st. It met BEA's needs almost exactly, but in the end the airline, under some Government pressure, ordered the smaller Trident 3B. The Two-Eleven was succeeded by the Three-Eleven, a wider-bodied development with two more powerful RB.211-61s and seating 233 passengers eight-abreast or up to 259 nine-abreast. BEA backed the Three-Eleven up to the hilt and would have had an initial requirement for 20 but this, too did not get the go-ahead.

Below:
Developed in parallel with the Series 700 was the Series 800 with two 22,000lb st SNECMA/GEC CFM 56 turbofans and seating from 144 to 161 passengers in a fuselage no less than 32ft 6in longer than the Series 500's. Span would have been 10ft greater, with a new centre-section.

It was the Rolls-Royce bankruptcy of 1970 that, more than almost any single event, probably stunted the One-Eleven's future development prospects, for the need to rescue Rolls and the ever larger sums consumed thereafter by the RB.211 family of engines inevitably gave a lower priority and poorer prospects to any of the refanned Speys that were proposed for developments like the One-Eleven 700. But above all, official thinking was still obsessed by the abstract idea of the size of industrial units, and did not pay nearly enough attention to what they manufactured or sold, and the importance of planning ahead. Several important mergers of this time were later widely regretted, in particular that between BOAC and BEA to form British Airways. This left a legacy of expensive overmanning that lasted for years, and resulted in BOAC's pro-American attitudes to new aircraft orders being allowed to eclipse BEA's determined and successful sponsorship of new British types, of which the Viscount was the most important example.